HOW TO RIG
AN ELECTION

Confessions of a
Republican Operative

ALLEN RAYMOND

WITH IAN SPIEGELMAN

SIMON & SCHUSTER PAPERBACKS

NEW YORK - LONDON - TORONTO - SYDNEY

SIMON & SCHUSTER PAPERBACKS
A Division of Simon & Schuster, Inc.
1230 Avenue of the Americas
New York, NY 10020

First Simon & Schuster hardcover edition September 2008

SIMON & SCHUSTER PAPERBACKS and colophon are registered trademarks
of Simon & Schuster, Inc.

For information about special discounts for bulk purchases,
please contact Simon & Schuster Special Sales at
1-800-456-6798 or business@simonandschuster.com.

Designed by Jaime Putorti

Manufactured in the United States of America

10 9 8 7 6 5 4 3 2 1

The Library of Congress has cataloged the hardcover as follows:
Raymond, Allen.
    How to rig an election : confessions of a Republican operative / Allen Raymond
with Ian Spiegelman.
        p.   cm.
1. Elections—Corrupt practices—New Hampshire.   I. Spiegelman, Ian.
II. Title.

JK 1994.R39 2008
364.1'32409742—dc22
                                                    2007041857

ISBN-13: 978-1-4165-5222-2
ISBN-10:   1-4165-5222-7
ISBN-13: 978-1-4165-5223-9 (pbk)
ISBN-10:   1-4165-5223-5 (pbk)

For Elizabeth

"Now I know what love is." –Virgil

In the following pages I offer nothing more than simple facts, plain arguments, and common sense; and have no other preliminaries to settle with the reader, than that he will divest himself of prejudice and prepossession, and suffer his reason and his feelings to determine for themselves; that he will put *on*, or rather that he will not put *off*, the true character of a man, and generously enlarge his views beyond the present day.

—Thomas Paine, *Common Sense*

HOW TO RIG AN ELECTION

FOREWORD

FEBRUARY 8, 2005. 10:30 A.M.

U.S. DISTRICT COURT, NEW HAMPSHIRE.

The first sign of trouble at my sentencing hearing came when the judge cut off my lawyer in the middle of his statement.

"What about common sense!?" Judge Joseph DiClerico said, referring to me. "What about a personal moral compass?"

My lawyer had been making the point that I'd consulted an attorney before committing my crime, to ascertain if it was in fact a crime in the first place. That attorney, a legal advisor for the Republican Leadership Council—and before that the general counsel for the Federal Election Commission—hadn't thought so, but it obviously concerned him enough not to put it on paper. That didn't set off any alarm bells for me, however. Back in 2002, just about every Republican operative was so dizzy with power that if you could find two of us who could still tell the difference between politics and crime, you could probably have rubbed us together for fire as well.

In GOP circles in 2002 it seemed preposterous that anything you did to win an election could be considered a crime. For ten years I'd been making phone calls with the intent to manipulate voters; hell, I'd been handsomely rewarded for it. In my business, communication devices were all lethal weapons—and every fight was dirty.

The judge could prattle on all he wanted about my "moral compass" because he didn't understand that any compass that doesn't
lead a campaigner to victory is utterly useless in American electioneering. At worst, I saw my campaigning snafu in the New Hampshire general election as just some more political tomfoolery to cap
off a decade in which my party had gone from getting our asses
kicked out of Washington to treating all three branches of the federal government like our own personal amusement parks. It had
been no easy trick, but Bill Clinton had opened the door for us with
his '93 tax hike just after I'd gotten out of grad school with a master's
in political management. Who would have thought that we could
convince so many blue-collar workers that raising taxes primarily
on white-collar workers was intrinsically wicked enough that they
and other voters should give us both the House and the Senate? If
we could get elected by convincing our own hard-up constituents
that they were in the same boat as the rich, what *wouldn't* a voter believe? Those were heady times—and we were just getting started.

We spent the next eight years giving the truth such a furious
beating every time it showed its face that it eventually just stopped
coming around altogether. Candidates, voters, the press—no one
wanted anything to do with it. The reporters gave up asking serious
questions, the voters stopped reading past the headlines, and it was
a very cozy arrangement for everyone.

By the time I was working in presidential politics, a bunch of our
guys got together and pretty much stole the presidency. And the
voters? Hell, they were so offended that they actually voted to maintain our congressional majority in the 2002 election.

How could we commit a crime when we could do no wrong?

But my sentencing hearing was held in the winter of 2005, and
by then the country was starting to consider unfettered GOP rule
just a little bit disastrous. Even the guys who didn't expose under-
cover CIA operatives, proposition congressional pages, buddy up
with Enron, and send other people's children off to die in an impossible war wouldn't rat on the ones who did.

Everywhere you turned, so many Republicans were screwing up so outrageously that even the press wasn't afraid of them anymore. When some GOP fixer—even in the White House itself—did something wrong, reporters actually went ahead and put it on the news just as if the Bush administration hadn't done everything it could to stamp out any remaining traces of a free and open society. Given the changes in the political climate, Judge DiClerico of the United States District Court in New Hampshire certainly saw no reason to be timid with the likes of me.

Until the judge tore into me, I had been thinking I'd get nothing worse than a few months of home confinement, a bit of a break that could be used to catch up on some relaxing little projects around the house. From the second the FBI came to my door I'd done every thing they wanted, connecting all the dots between the shady tactics of the New Hampshire Republican Party during the John E. Sununu Senate campaign, the Bushie who'd orchestrated the whole thing, and me. The Department of Justice was getting ready to indict, because of my testimony, President George W. Bush's main political guy in New England. The DOJ went so far as to argue that I should be given the best possible treatment by the court for my exemplary cooperation. Why wouldn't I have cooperated? After all, when the shit hit the fan, my political party and my former colleagues not only threw me under the bus but then blamed me for getting run over.

After he finished with my lawyer, Judge DiClerico said, "I understand someone here wanted to make a statement."

Suddenly the chairman of the New Hampshire Democratic Party, Kathy Sullivan, popped up and spoke from the gallery. "What Mr. Raymond did was unforgivable," she said. "He assaulted democracy. It is a travesty that this could happen here at home, made all the worse by the fact that Iraqi citizens just had their purple thumbs in the air in triumph for having had their first free election."

The argument lacked reason, sure, but it was brimming with the broken bones, missing limbs, and body bags that give politics flavor when substance is in short supply. She did everything but glue a beard to my face and call me Saddam.

That would have been bad enough, but the judge followed up by calling on the most damning speaker of all. "Would the defendant like to address the court?"

Now I was truly screwed. I'd been given no warning that I'd be expected to speak, so I had nothing prepared. All of my political training dictated that you spend as much time as possible preparing for any eventuality and that there was only one thing to do if you were ever caught off guard: bullshit them.

But in the three years between my crime and my sentencing, all the bullshit had been thoroughly knocked out of me. My old pals at the Republican National Committee were spending almost $3 million on my coconspirator's legal defense because he was still a loyal member of the GOP family, while at the same time labeling me a liar, a rogue, and a thief to any news outlet that would listen. From former bosses to business partners, colleagues to clients, the Party Elite couldn't lie about me fast enough, and they didn't send a dime of Republican defense money my way even though I'd served the cause for its entire glorious decade, from the Contract with America to taking back the White House.

What was I going to say? "You can't trust these guys—I should know, I used to work with them!" The idea of spinning my own trial—the idea of spinning anything ever again—made me feel sick. For both the Democrats and the Republicans, this trial, my trial, was merely another campaign. But it was my reputation, my family, my life.

The experience left me a spirited proponent of the truth.

Standing there, withering under the judge's glare, all I could think of was being a little kid and having my mother tell me that when you did something bad, you had to apologize.

"Your Honor," I said, "I did a bad thing."

He looked at me like I was just giving him more of the spin my indictment had generated in the press, like I was still the same full-of-shit GOP operative I'd been since I first hit the ground politically. But this was me, to the bone, and maybe that was the saddest part. After a decade of slashing and burning my way up the ranks of American politics to become a high-level Republican Party campaign op and then a highly compensated Republican political consultant, I stood in that courtroom in all of my natural glory: a privileged, newly minted felon who had spent a career carefully massaging ideas into messages but who now couldn't string together a couple of coherent sentences.

I tried again.

"It was a terrible endeavor to undertake. While what I did was outside of my character, I take full responsibility for those actions. I apologize to the court and to the people of New Hampshire."

In the next national election cycle, Republicans would be apologizing to towns and cities and states all across America, but for the first time in thirteen years I'd have nothing to do with who won those elections. After serving out the sentence the judge was about to impose on me, I wouldn't even be allowed to vote.

ONE

*T*hough I come from a rather illustrious old American family, politics was certainly not in my blood. In fact, until I became an operative for the Republican Party in the early 1990s, my family had managed to steer clear of that dirty business ever since a relative, Hentry Jarvis Raymond, cofounded the Republican Party and my great-great-grandfather, Darwin Rush James, retired from Congress in 1887. My maternal great-grandfather was the printer and entrepreneur John Thomas Underwood, who cofounded the Underwood Typewriter Company, whose products bore one of the great brands in American history. When I was a kid, I could open any closet in any family home and find one of his ancient machines gathering dust. His wife, my great-grandmother Nana, was the kind of classic Yankee matriarch who would refer to people by what they manufactured, saying things like "Singer, they're in sewing machines." It amused her when the electrician hung a light over the wrong masterpiece. "No, no," she had laughed, "the *other* Monet!"

Of course that was a few generations ago, and my mother always used that old anecdote as an object lesson in how not to conduct myself. It was her considered opinion that the privileged came in two classes: the ones who worked hard to understand the true value of things, and the foolish.

While the Underwood fortune ensured that I'd never go hungry, family pride—hell, my own pride—ensured that I'd never be some yacht-hopping scion whose only full-time employment consisted of finding increasingly undignified ways to wrinkle his linen suits. Still, figuring out what I might do with my life was a tricky prospect. My paternal grandfather, Allen Raymond, had been a legendary correspondent for the *New York Times, New York Herald,* and the *International Herald Tribune,* so I had always been very aware of current events, particularly politics. But having spent my youth around an endless succession of reporters, I knew too much about them to ever become one myself.

The first thing I tried when I got out of college in 1989 was public relations, working for a New York firm at $21,000 a year. The Underwood money sure came in handy those days, since I was probably spending about $35,000 a year. The money wasn't a big issue for me, but after two years it was clear enough that I wasn't going to make much of an impact on the world doing flack work for BMW and Toshiba. My college buddies were on their way to significant careers in finance, one running the oil trade desk for Morgan Stanley, another trading his own capital from the family seat on the New York Stock Exchange, while I was going nowhere. I wanted to do something remarkable, to leave my imprint somehow. Here I had this legacy that was an American institution and I could never shake the feeling that I had to find some way to measure up to it.

The one thing I found interesting about PR work was that it challenged you to manipulate people's perceptions. Instead of dealing in cold, hard facts, you had supple, yielding elements that you could present in whatever way best suited your needs. Reality was malleable—it could be made to bend to your will. What, for instance, could the Super Bowl possibly have to do with toilet cleanser? Nothing at all, unless you happened to be the low man on the Ty-D-Bol account, as I was. It seemed a pretty stupid task to me when I spent weeks and weeks gathering data to find out how many gallons of water Americans flushed during the big game each year. But it was suddenly a brilliant bit of mind control when the Super Bowl announcers were discussing my statistics and my client during halftime at the most highly viewed sporting event of the year.

The idea that you could massage people's perceptions so that they saw what you wanted them to see fascinated me. I didn't exactly have a stranglehold on what my own reality even was at the time, but that didn't seem a very big deal. I just knew that if the little bit of mental sleight of hand I'd learned could be expanded upon, I could make something happen. What that was, precisely, I had no idea.

Becoming a salesman seemed an obvious choice, but for a salesman to leave a substantial footprint on the world he needs a pretty extraordinary product. When I failed to locate such a product in my own imagination, I thought I might find it in higher education; I started looking around at grad schools. None of the programs jumped out at me until I came across an ad for a new one-year program at Baruch College called the Graduate School of Political Management (GSPM). "Political management"—not that I knew what that actually meant, but it sounded cool. With all my youthful anxiety about living up to my heritage, with the full weight of our moneyed history bearing down on me, that's really all the thought I ended up giving the matter: "Politics. That sounds cool." Well, that and, "I'll give it a shot."

If the notion that a politician is little more than a product pitched by salesmen had dawned on me at the time, it was entirely on a subconscious level.

Fortunately for me, the program was only two years old at the time, and its admissions department was still desperate for people who could pay their way in with fifteen grand. It wasn't like getting into Harvard Law by a long shot—more like getting into community college. (The program did end up moving to George Washington University in Washington, D.C., and has become quite a well-respected institution since I passed through its doors.)

At that time, the Graduate School of Political Management wasn't physically impressive, either. The school occupied a quarter of a floor in a run-down building near City Hall in New York. Literally shoved in a corner, it consisted of a large conference room, two small classrooms, and some staff offices. The rooms smelled moldy, the chairs were broken. What I'd come to learn later is that, at almost every level of American campaigning, low-rent, dank, and dismal is the default setting for all accommodations.

We were a small class, maybe thirty-five students altogether, and my attitude toward the program shifted from give-it-a-shot to win-at-all-costs on day one. High-profile internships for the likes of Roger Ailes and the legendary Democratic image-maker Hank Sheinkopf were being dangled in front of the class and, for a lot of us, the sense of competition was immediately apparent. Unlike college, which hadn't been about much of anything, performance here promised real rewards in the real world.

Just sitting there in our seats it was obvious that everyone was sizing one another up. At orientation, I remember feeling like I was older than the rest of the class by at least three years chronologically, and by a decade in terms of real work experience. Most of my classmates seemed to think this was just an extension of their senior year in college, while I felt like the experience was laying the groundwork for the rest of my life. I was, after all, the only person in the room wearing a suit.

If this is my competition in this industry, I thought, I've got it made. At the same time, I still had a nagging doubt as to whether I was doing the right thing. This felt more to me like learning a trade than entering a profession, as if I'd just spent $15,000 to go to Apex Tech. It was a totally blind gamble for me.

As I scanned the room, nobody looked like anyone I'd want to hang out with. I was just there to go to class and try to start a career, not to make friends. But that was a major flaw in my personality, since half of politics is basic networking or, more precisely, kissing ass. To this day I wonder how much further I might have gone in the industry if I'd managed to add that ability to my skill set.

When it came time for each of us to introduce ourselves to the class, a big flamboyant girl with about two coats of makeup on stood up from her chair and announced, "I'm from Arkansas and Bill Clinton is going to be the next president of the United States!"

We all essentially responded, "You're crazy!" We immediately dismissed her as a potential rival—she was clearly an overly emotional type.

Back then Clinton was nobody. This was three months before Iowa, four months before New Hampshire, and George H. W. Bush still had an 80 percent approval rating from the war in Iraq that wasn't a horrible misstep that will haunt our country for generations to come. But sure enough, the brassy girl from Arkansas turned out to be spot-on.

Of course that was a total fluke, a rare occurrence of naïve, hometown bravado lining up with actual events. But what I didn't know then, and it became one of the most important political lessons I'd ever learn, is that once you can spot the patterns in politics your predictions are usually going to be dead to rights. I first witnessed this kind of genuine political divination when our dean, Chris Arterton, correctly predicted that Bush would bring back Jim Baker to run his campaign. To us tyros it was an absurd notion that Ronald Reagan's chief of staff and treasury secretary, who was then serving as President George H. W. Bush's secretary of state, would leave that post to take the reins of the forty-first president's reelection campaign. George H. W. Bush had the aura of invincibility and none of us believed a guru like Baker would need to be called back into campaign service. Two months later it turned out to be true.

What Arterton had done is nothing you can learn in school, though. You have to have your own skin in the game. At the time, all of us students merely talked as if we did. But once you have skin in the game, you don't need to talk anymore—you're too worried about your skin. As impressed as I was with Arterton, my whole reason for being at GSPM was to work my way into the presence of true political giants. My first exposure to a real power player came when Roger Ailes showed up as a guest lecturer. Ailes had just taken over CNBC, which meant nothing to us, but he'd played a key role in getting Bush elected over Michael Dukakis in 1988, and his book, *You Are the Message: Secrets of the Master Communicators,* was a must-read for our class, along with Sun-Tzu's *The Art of War,* Machiavelli's *The Prince,* and Carl von Clausewitz's *On War.*

Ailes was larger than life, and not just because he's got a gut like the hood of a VW Bug. This was the guy who dreamed up the town hall forum for Richard Nixon, and who saved Bush's ass in '88. This guy was Lee Atwater's Lee Atwater. He personified what everyone in that room wanted to be.

What we wanted—what *I* wanted, whether I truly knew it at the time or not, was the worst thing anyone could want, and the thing most people never stop chasing: power. Wealth, health, youth . . . I had those in spades. All I lacked was influence over other human beings. Now *there* was something worth having!

Ailes walked in and I thought, I want to be a guy who, when the door closes and there're only three people left in the room, is one of them. When something needs to happen and it takes a man of influence in a dark room to make it happen, I want to be that man. Once Ailes began his lecture, no one said a thing. The man's whole attitude was "I'm gonna talk and you're gonna listen. I'm going to lay it down for you and if you don't pick it up, hey, that's your loss."

What he laid down for us was simply this: in politics, words are meaningless.

It isn't what you say, but how you say it. Every aspect of the phrases a candidate spews forth are insignificant except for how he emotes them. For better or worse, we've seen it proved countless times in the last ten years that Ailes's theory is accurate—not right or wrong, but *accurate*.

And we all saw that accuracy soon enough with Bill Clinton's "I feel your pain" message. That line would have seemed smarmy to almost anyone if they'd read it in campaign literature, but Clinton embodied the theme so skillfully when he delivered it at a March 1992 campaign rally that it resonated perfectly with millions of voters.

I had personally marveled at Clinton's ability to stay on message that January, when he deftly outmaneuvered *60 Minutes* correspondent Steve Kroft over tabloid stories alleging an affair with Gennifer Flowers. The masterstroke wasn't when he blamed it on checkbook journalism, saying, "It was only when money came out, when the tabloids went down there offering people money to say that they had been involved with me, that she changed her story." The genius move was that he immediately added, "There's a recession going on." In ten seconds Bill Clinton went from denying a sordid sex tale to bashing President Bush on the economy. But more than that, he was actually *blaming* Bush's recession for poor Gennifer Flowers having to debase herself in the press. In this way Clinton got back to the message "It's the economy, stupid," dismissed Flowers as a gold digger, and delivered it all with an air of compassion for his accuser that would satisfy the liberal female voters he needed to win the election.

Bill Clinton may not have agreed with any of Roger Ailes's politics, but he certainly sounded like he'd read Ailes's book.

I came away from Ailes's lecture with the distinct impression that I'd enlisted in a military academy. He had the presence and bearing of a movie general as he drummed home the message that if you didn't personally believe what you were spinning, you'd damned well better work yourself into a lather until you looked and sounded like you did—that if you were ever to be a true political player, you had to indoctrinate *yourself.* And I felt myself growing fully indoctrinated. In fact, GSPM's Web site still refers to the school as "The West Point of Politics." When you're young you can really get into that. You think to yourself, I'm a badass gunslinger, when in truth you're just a privileged white kid who's never seen the inside of a brawl. But you get sucked into that bravado before you've even hit the ground and done anything. And that attitude only grows with the confidence success brings; the higher you go in politics, in either party, the more pervasive it is—the more childish and just plain stupid.

The class that would prove most valuable to me in my career (and, in a way, end it) was a phone polling course taught by Barbara Farah, who was formerly Director of News Surveys at *The New York Times*. When she asked us to draft a survey, I figured I was way ahead of the game thanks to some PR work I'd done for Toshiba involving the U.S.-Japanese trade issue. When I'd given Barbara what I considered to be a deeply thought-out, intricate poll on our commercial relations with Japan, she took one look and told me, "You've got to dumb this down to the second grade. This is way too complex for your average voter."

A little taken aback, I asked, "Huh?"

"People are just too busy," she explained. "No one has time to pay attention to anything. You need to dumb this down to 'Dim, dem, and dose.' "

The lesson, and no one says you have to like it, is: If you want to succeed for your candidate, or as a candidate, you cannot be above the general public's comprehension. And the general public's comprehension is pretty low.

Another assignment was to conduct an actual telephone poll, for which we were supplied with a script and a selection of random telephone numbers for voters throughout the five boroughs of New York. I still have that script. When I had completed the assignment, I wrote on it, "Despite the proliferation of telecommunications in the U.S., many people remain afraid to use the phone. What I learned was never to be afraid to use the phone to retrieve or communicate information."

To retrieve or communicate information . . . If only I'd stuck strictly to those two telephonic applications when I was working the phones in New Hampshire, what a different story I'd be telling.

The course was called "Quantitative Methods," but its subject matter wasn't as dry as the name implied. For our polling project we had to call through our list of numbers until we had done six complete interviews. All of my numbers were in Queens and I ended up experiencing a language barrier on about 75 percent of my calls. At the time, we were applying our studies to the New York mayoral rematch between Rudy Giuliani and David Dinkins, so our scripts revolved around that race. The questions were fairly straightforward: "Who are you most likely to vote for?" and such. Yet I soon found myself coaxing my subjects through the interviews. It wasn't so much that I was trying to assign particular responses to the subjects, but I realized it was incredibly easy to lead someone into giving any answer you wanted.

The key was when I'd pose a simple question and the respondent would ask, "What does that mean?" Once they asked what something meant, I could just go ahead and rephrase it any way I chose because the script didn't provide any answers, only more questions.

Ideally, you're supposed to say, "I can't tell you what it means. I can only read you the question." But no one's ever been elected on ideals. What you end up telling them is more along the lines of "Well, what I think it means is A, and based on your income level and the other demographics in your file you'd be most likely to answer B."

This was a real eye-opener. This was where the rubber meets the road. If you can twist polling results, you can use those same results to manipulate everything from fund-raising to media perception. What had started out as an innocuous exercise in "quantitative methods"—polling and the retrieval of information via the phone—became my first lesson in wedge politics.

In wedge politics, you're trying to polarize just enough of a given electorate to get your candidate the win. You don't care about 100 percent of the vote; you don't even care about 55 percent of it. In wedge politics, you want to get 50 percent, plus one vote. If you can find an issue that turns off 49 percent of the voters, your guy gets 51 percent and you win. "Quantitative methods" is about using the polls to find—or, better yet, create—the negative issue that turns off the right segment of voters. That's Wedge Politics.

And American politics is Wedge Politics.

And that's only the beginning of what political operatives can do when they reach into someone's home armed with a telephone, a few loaded questions, and the Second Amendment.

Through the Giuliani-Dinkins race I saw firsthand that there was an art and a science to phone polling. It struck me that this was not a race about budgets, education, and crime, but how those issues impacted different racial groups. At the time, New York seemed ready to burst from racial tension and an ever-increasing crime rate. As the white candidate in that dynamic, Giuliani had no shot with black voters. But Latino and white voters were fertile ground for him even if they were Democrats in one of the nation's most liberal cities. Simply put, high crime rates and racial tension equaled frightened, angry white people. Giuliani's camp responded to this with one message, one vision: "Rudy is tough on crime; Dinkins doesn't care if whitey gets mugged."

In that atmosphere, when the Republicans reportedly had men with "inner-city" accents call Democratic households urging "Vote for David Dinkins," they were betting that white Democrats would turn out for Rudy. At least that's how I understood it as an engaged observer.

Was the tactic dirty? Was it clean? Meaningless. It was victorious.

Race-based electioneering through phone polling was abso-

lutely tame, however, compared to the lengths that earlier operatives had gone to in order to manipulate the polls. In 1981, the
Republican National Committee (RNC) birthed the modern-day
voter suppression tactic in New Jersey. The RNC, in conjunction
with the New Jersey Republican State Committee (NJGOP), dis-
couraged minority voters from showing up at the polls by hiring off-
duty law-enforcement officers to stand at urban polling places
wearing black armbands that identified them as members of the
nonexistent "Ballot Security Task Force." With their sidearms clearly
visible, they stood next to signs that read: "WARNING. This area is
being controlled by the National Ballot Security Task Force. It is a
crime to falsify a ballot or to violate election laws."

That year Republican Tom Kean, Sr., defeated Democrat Jim
Florio for governor by 1,797 votes. The criminal investigation went
nowhere and the ensuing civil suit against the RNC and NJGOP
ended up being settled for one dollar in U.S. district court. Both
committees signed a pledge never to approve tactics that would intimidate voters—but did not admit wrongdoing.

A theme on which we were ceaselessly drilled at the GSPM was
that the candidate who asks "Is it fair to get me elected this way?"
is the candidate who's never won. When a nonmilitary educational
institution's primary reading list is composed of Sun-Tzu, Ailes,
Clausewitz, and Machiavelli, you can bet its ethics are going to be
something special. Professor Bob Fullinwider of the University of
Maryland's Institute for Philosophy and Public Policy was our go-to
guy on that front. The cover page on the syllabus for his "Ethics and
Politics" course featured two quotes:

"Politics is a blood sport."
—Edward I. Koch

*"The credit belongs to the man who is actually in the arena,
whose face is marred by dust and sweat and blood, who strives
valiantly, who errs and comes up short again and again, who*

*knows the great enthusiasm, the great devotion, who spends him-
self in a worthy cause. And if he fails, at least he fails while daring greatly, knowing that he will never be with those cold, timid
souls who knew neither victory nor defeat."*
　　　　　　　　　　　　　—*Teddy Roosevelt*

Be good, be bad, but don't be indifferent—that was the frame-
work. Be competitive, be in the sport. From there on in, all the gam-
ing strategies we studied were war strategies, battlefield tactics.

Years later, I went to Angola as a representative of the International Republican Institute to teach members of an emerging democracy about what a democracy is and how it works. They didn't
understand what I was saying about electoral politics until I started
equating it with warfare. When I said that TV ads are the political
equivalent of carpet bombing while a telephone pollster is a sniper,
only then did the heads start nodding.

All the warfare stuff we were trained in served to bolster one
philosophy: win or go home. As for what political fixers considered
ethical in getting the win, that was made clear to me at GSPM when
I was introduced to the American Association of Political Consultants. A speaker from the AAPC gave a lecture, which he opened
by handing out copies of the association's code of ethics.

The first oath on the list read, "I shall not indulge in any activity that would corrupt or degrade the practice of political campaigning."

"Of course, I don't pay too much attention to that," the speaker
said, "as I'm not a dues-paying member anyway."

So to me, the message was "Ethics this, fair play that—it's all
bullshit. You lose, you go home. You win, you win."

It was then I learned the Golden Rule: he who has the gold
makes the rules.

The Maryland professor aside, most of the people who taught
us weren't academics by any stretch. They were from the down-
and-dirty world of political operatives and they were tasked with

teaching us the down-and-dirty realities of lobbying, polling, budgeting, and advertising, just to mention the basics. By the time I left GSPM I felt like I'd just been trained to be a mercenary. I just got out of boot camp and it was time to go annihilate someone.

At the same time, I couldn't help asking myself, "Dude, you just spent fifteen thousand dollars. What do you do now?"

I knew what I wanted to do, but had little idea of how to go about doing it.

TWO

When I got my degree I was twenty-three years old, and despite my youth, I found it impossible to be fanatically for or against any sociopolitical issue. To me the differences between Republicans and Democrats were negligible; I was ready to work for either party—all that mattered to me was finding that work. For all I had learned at the Graduate School of Political Management, it hadn't taught me much about where to look for a political job or even what kind of jobs there were to look for. So I ended up reaching out for advice to a classmate named Keith White, a well-connected Democrat whose sister had been a classmate of mine at Hobart and William Smith Colleges.

As far as choosing which party to work for, Keith settled that issue for me when he pointed out the most crucial factor.

"The Republicans are on the rise," he said. "That's where all the money's heading."

We were having lunch in New York and I nearly choked on my sushi. In the first place, White and his family were major players in the Democratic machine. In the second, I'd never eaten sushi before.

I knew that my grad school degree wasn't intrinsically worth a hell of a lot, but I had held out some hope that it would at least save me from having to start at the absolute bottom of the campaign pecking order. White quickly disabused me of that notion.

"Okay," I said, "but what's the bottom? What's that look like? How deep does it go?"

"It's probably sticking up yard signs in some out-of-the-way county somewhere. When I said the bottom I wasn't kidding."

So I had that to look forward to. But where?

"What about the mayoral race?" I asked. "Can I get in on that?"

"Probably not. Giuliani already ran against Dinkins. He lost, but he's already got an operation in place and it's going to be hard to break into it. Plus, you'd have to live in New York City and the cost of living isn't going down. Your burn rate's going to be pretty high if you're between campaigns and you're living here."

"Where else am I going to live?"

Very matter-of-factly, White told me, "You should be a New Jersey Republican. They have elections every year, so they're always looking for talented guys. Besides, you're fiscally conservative and they've got a Democratic governor who just raised taxes, which means that every Republican running already has the polarizing issue."

The New Jersey idea gelled for me almost instantly. New Jersey was probably the only place in the world where I could show up and honestly say, "I'm *from* here." My mother was something of a rolling stone. All my life, we uprooted to a new city or country every five years—first relocating from Manhattan to California, and after that to France. But the one constant throughout was that I spent every summer at the beach house my great-grandfather built on the Jersey Shore. So I grew up there as much as anywhere.

I could show up in a candidate's office and be "Al Raymond from Bay Head," a hometown guy, not some carpetbagger who parachuted in looking for work. There was no other place where I could get away with that.

I tried it out on Keith, saying, "You know, I actually did grow up on the Jersey Shore."

"Great!" he said. "Use that! That puts people at ease a little bit, because politics is a very parochial thing, especially at the state level. You meet someone and the first thing they want to know is, 'Who are you? You're a stranger.' But if you tell them, 'No, I'm so-and-so, and I know so-and-so,' they'll start to catalog you in their minds. The bar comes down a little."

So now it was decided: I was a Republican from the great state of New Jersey. All that was left was to actually become that thing.

— — —

My first job was about as close to the bottom as you can get in politics and still get paid. I was hired to be the regional coordinator for Bush/Quayle '92 in three New Jersey counties. But I didn't actually work for Bush/Quayle '92, I worked for "Victory '92." The "Victory" programs were Republican Party–sponsored organizations that ran parallel to the real campaign. So in the counties of Sussex, Bergen, and Hudson, I was in charge of every campaign-related issue that didn't actually involve the candidates, their campaign advisors, or, at any truly meaningful level, the campaign itself.

My job was to organize volunteers, write letters to the editors of the most local of local newspapers, knock on doors, and, as Keith White had warned, put up dozens and dozens of lawn signs. My master's degree meant shit. It didn't matter if I was years ahead of my position in terms of knowledge; I still had to go ahead and get my ticket punched. I was so low on the ladder I had to stretch to reach the first rung.

Meanwhile, I was still having a pretty good time, living in a two-bedroom on the Upper East Side with a college buddy, reverse-commuting into Jersey every morning in my Volkswagen Passat, working hard, and going out every once in a while.

Mine may not have been the most important position in the

organization, but it was always interesting. The three counties I covered were vastly different from one another. Hudson was a Democratic stronghold, Sussex was GOP land, and Bergen, the quintessential swing county, was up for grabs. Depending on the time of day, I'd find myself in enemy territory, on safe ground, or in no-man's-land. One day I would be meeting with a bunch of Cuban exiles in Hudson, the next it was farmers and gun nuts in Sussex, and then to a luncheon with a group of Carmela Soprano types in Bergen.

I was working out of the Bergen County Republican Organization's offices in Hackensack because they were midway between Hudson and Sussex counties. The way I saw it, there wasn't much I could do in Hudson with the Dems pretty much owning it, but Lee Lichtenberger, an insurance man who was also the Hudson County Republican chair, insisted on showing me around the area anyway.

Hudson County is basically the Miami of New Jersey. If you're a Hudson Republican, you're probably Cuban. So Lee arranged a meeting for me with a few local Cuban businessmen. Before the big sit-down, though, he gave me a rather mysterious set of instructions.

"Whatever you do," he said, "don't say anything. Just clam up. I know what you want, so I'll speak for you, but I'll make it seem like I'm just doing what you're telling me to do. If I ask you a question, just nod or shake your head."

"Why?"

"And don't commit to giving any money," he went on, ignoring me. "If they ask you for money, just look at them and say, 'I don't talk about money.' Oh, and wear a trench coat. Keep your hands in the pockets and look serious."

"Listen," I tried again, "why am I doing all that?"

"Just trust me. I know these guys. I know how they think."

I was new to the business—so as weird as it all sounded, maybe this was the way everyone operated at the grassroots level. I wasn't going to make a fuss.

The meet was held at a little restaurant on Bergenline Avenue in Union City. After I'd eaten my first-ever Cuban sandwich, the discussion started—in Spanish. I kept my mouth shut, hands in pockets, with what I hoped looked like a serious expression on my face. Initially, I thought Lee was keeping me quiet to avoid some kind of social faux pas. But it started to dawn on me that something entirely different—and not nearly so innocent—was going on.

When we got back in Lee's car, I asked him, "So are you going to tell me what the hell that was all about?"

"That?" he shrugged. "I just told the guys you were CIA."

"Dude, you told them *what*?"

"These guys never do what I tell them to do, but now that they think you're CIA they'll do anything I want."

And they did. After that lunch everyone who'd attended put up their own money and we opened a hole-in-the-wall Victory '92 headquarters right there on Bergenline Avenue. That little outpost in Democratic territory ended up being important. When Dorothy "Doro" Bush Koch, daughter of George H. W. Bush, visited Hudson County, we managed to turn out a few hundred people to cheer for her and we scored a lot of press, which wasn't an easy trick to pull off in the enemy's backyard.

Still, to land my job you basically had to have a pulse and look like you could drive a car without getting a traffic ticket. As far as the New Jersey Republican Party was concerned, I was no one from nowhere. To the Republican National Committee, I was even less than that. But I was building up my Rolodex every day. You never know exactly whom you might be meeting. They might not be important today, but tomorrow it could be an entirely different story.

County chairs, committee people, other candidates, other operatives—I was constantly taking numbers and taking people out for drinks. At some point my name must have made it up the channels, because when Marilyn Quayle decided to stop by the swing county of Bergen for a fund-raiser and her people wanted a crowd of a hundred supporters to receive her at the airport, who did they call?

I knew before she even touched down that the airport event was going to be a monster of a flop because most of the local pols weren't even interested in turning up. When Barbara Bush had come into New Jersey a month before, I'd witnessed dozens of fully grown and otherwise reasonable Party ops bickering like little kids over who would get the few precious all-access Secret Service security pins that were available for the event. They were groupies looking for backstage passes so they could score a second of face time with the First Lady. I made great use of my own pin, by the way; when Barbara Bush's advance person introduced us in the lobby at the event, I tried to say, "It's an honor to meet you," but ended up mumbling it so pathetically that the First Lady said, "What are you trying to say?" and looked at me as if I was an idiot before she walked away. At that point in my career, being face-to-face with a candidate's wife was the closest I'd ever come to actually meeting a candidate. For the rest of my career, I would try to avoid my clients' spouses whenever possible—they always reminded me of the candidate's humanity, which hampered my ability to remain cold and calculating.

Barbara Bush was hardly an endearing figure, but she was still the First Lady of the United States, and any Party hack could see the value of simply being able to snap a picture with her. Marilyn Quayle, however, didn't even have that going for her. Even within the Party, Dan Quayle was considered such a dimwit that we suspected a double-secret alternative succession plan existed in case anything ever happened to Bush. As soon as I got the call from Mrs. Quayle's people informing me that I was expected to drum up a hundred warm, enthusiastic bodies to be at the airport at noon on a Tuesday, I hung up and asked myself, "Who the fuck are they kidding?"

When the plane arrived at Teterboro, fifteen people were there to greet the Second Lady. Ten of them were waving Clinton/Gore signs that they'd somehow sneaked into the event.

I remembered my grad school classmate from Arkansas, the big gaudy girl who stood up on the first day to proclaim that Bill Clinton would be the next president, and how me and the other robots had laughed at her. That had been in the fall of 1991, and now here it was the summer of 1992 and Marilyn Quayle couldn't draw enough people to fill a city bus—not even a crowd of jeerers.

It's one thing to be a divisive political figure; it's another thing when no one even cares enough to show up to tell you how much they hate you.

It was clear: Clinton was going to kick Bush's ass.

I was mortified. Not because Bush was finished, but because my career had just started and it was already cratering. Of course no one above me had bothered to send out any letters about the Quayle event or make any phone calls. But as new as I was to politics, I wasn't so new that I thought that fact would get me off the hook.

What did save me, frankly, was that the Bush campaign wasn't faring much better anywhere else. It was dying all over. The only thing anyone working for it could do was keep collecting paychecks while it lasted and start looking for their next gig. I was doing just that in the back office at the Bergen County Republican Organization when I heard this huge commotion coming from up front.

People were yelling and screaming like the place was on fire. Setting campaign offices on fire wasn't at all unheard of in local politics, by the way, so I ran up front as a few of my coworkers ran past me in the opposite direction.

Four guys dressed like Hamas militants, faces covered in patterned balaclavas, were trashing the place and screaming at the top of their lungs. Desks and tables were being flipped over, filing cabinets had been knocked down, spilling papers all over the floor, and an office copier lay on its face, buzzing and grinding its gears in the dust.

I took a second to screw up some courage, then yelled, "Hey! Who the fuck are you? What the fuck are you doing here?"

In response they started chanting, "Kahane Chai! Kahane Chai!"

"What does that mean? What are you saying?"

One of them took a break from ransacking the office to inform me, "We have bombs! We're taking hostages! Who's in charge?"

I decided immediately that they didn't need that information. Pointing to the next room, I shouted, "The person in charge is in there!"

Like some kind of cartoon terrorists, they actually ran right into the other office. Before they realized that they were alone in there, I slammed the door behind them and tipped a filing cabinet in front of it. One office must have been as good as another to them, because they quickly ignored the blocked door and proceeded to smash everything around them. By the time a bunch of Hackensack cops came running in a minute later, the guys were starting to sound like caged animals.

Of the ten cops on the scene, the shortest, fattest one in the bunch was picked to go in. He took off his hat, drew his gun, and, lowering his head and shoulders like a pit bull, told me, "You gotta get out of here."

I was happy to oblige. It turned out the attackers were followers of the controversial Israeli nationalist and Jewish Defense League founder Rabbi Meir David Kahane, who had been assassinated in Manhattan two years before. What that had to do with the Bergen County headquarters of Victory '92, I still have no idea. But in a society where one vote is all the say most people will ever have over the way their own country is operated, an election can take on monstrous proportions. People start to get the strange idea that their government has nothing whatsoever to do with them and, when that happens, elections can make them do the craziest things.

Whatever sent those maniacs to my office, this new life of mine was a far cry from the dreary existence that PR work had provided for me in New York. It didn't matter that I got paid virtually nothing—the excitement alone was reward enough! The Victory '92 campaign was a dog, to be sure, but being front and center as Jewish terrorists wrecked my headquarters had an edge to it that told me running campaigns was only going to get better.

On Election Day I was given a $15,000 cash slush fund by the New Jersey Republican State Committee to pay the supposedly unpaid "volunteers." These were Party stalwarts who worked as poll watchers; kids we recruited to go door to door handing out literature; and the people who drove them around to the targeted houses. After paying them off and treating the gang to food and drinks, I pocketed a $2,000 bonus for myself.

The idea of handing out an untraceable wad of bills for people to do what are generally considered common civic duties hardly seemed unusual to me. At GSPM, I had studied how John F. Kennedy's campaign team overcame anti-Catholic prejudice in Protestant West Virginia by giving voters cash in exchange for going to the polls in the 1960 Democratic primary. The West Virginia win, and the money that bought it, cinched the national nomination for Kennedy and put Hubert Humphrey out of business.

George Bush had no such luck.

The violent death of Victory '92's headquarters was a more vigorous and interesting end than that of the Bush campaign, which finally just wandered off like an old sick animal looking for a cool, shady place to die. Me, I was still young and the picture of health, looking for a good place to work.

THREE

I knew there'd be plenty of job opportunities in January when all the candidates in the statewide elections started hiring their campaign staffs, but it was only November when my stint with Victory '92 had finished up and I needed to find some work in the meantime. A guy I'd gotten friendly with during the Bush/Quayle death march, Pat Torpey, had become the political director for New Jersey's Assembly Republican Majority, the campaign arm of the GOP's drive to win seats in the lower house of the state legislature. It sounds rinky-dink—until one considers that in 1993 the state's budget was $15.6 billion and that the legislators in the assembly and senate controlled that money. Pat was overseeing all the assembly campaigns for the Republicans and he told me the New Jersey Republican State Committee was looking for an opposition research director. Pat set me up with a job interview.

An opposition research director is the eager operative who digs through the trash in search of useful info about the competition. The information can be anything from a dirty secret to a perfectly innocent and aboveboard action, which you then turn into a dirty secret through political circumlocution and sleight of hand: six of one, half a dozen of the other. Find just one little screwup in your opponent's past—or any little thing you can turn into a screwup—and you can not only win the election, but also end a career. In any case, I really wanted that job—it was the sole remaining Republican position that needed to be filled in New Jersey.

My interview with Bill Ulrey, the executive director of the Republican State Committee, was conducted over lunch at Lorenzo's Restaurant in Trenton. Lorenzo's was ground zero for the Garden State's top lobbyists and power players, a wood-paneled joint that tried to exude old-world clubbiness in a town that, at the time, had the atmosphere of an industrial accident. Nonetheless, Lorenzo's mystique wasn't lost on me when I was sitting down across the table from Ulrey.

That lunch was the only instance in my career that I so much as mentioned GSPM. Basically, I told Ulrey, "I have a master's degree; I want the job."

Just like that, I went from running three counties for a nebulous phantom organization to working at the heart of the machine itself, the establishment. My job was two-pronged: to help the Republicans win seats in the state legislature, not by running them directly against their Democratic rivals, but by running them against the state's already vilified Democratic governor; and to wear away what little political cache that governor had left in advance of the gubernatorial election.

Governor Jim Florio was up for reelection and he was taking a beating because he had been elected in 1989 on his promise (he'd tell you it was a rumination) not to raise taxes, but had then raised them to the tune of $2.8 billion in 1990. His excuse was that he hadn't seen any reason to raise taxes while running for office in '89 but that once he'd gotten a look at things from the inside, he saw that everyone had been cooking the books. According to Florio he didn't have any choice.

It was a reasonable explanation, and just the kind of thing that gets a politician ridden out of office on a rail.

My mission as opposition research director was to craft as big a rail as possible. Whatever Florio's reasons, he had said A and done B; he was ripe to be defined by his opponents. And that definition was unavoidable: hypocrite.

At heart, my job was simply to remind the press of that "hypocrisy" at every opportunity, to keep generating document after document that supported the Republican refrain of "Jim Florio says one thing but does another."

Some campaigns require a scalpel and fine motor skills, while others demand a hatchet. This was a hatchet job.

In opposition research, what you're always going for is the info-slam. When you attack your opponent you want to support it with so much documentation that it's an anvil of paper. The attack itself might consist of a single sentence, but the supporting documents can be a stack of paper fifty pages high.

When a reporter calls to ask you to back up your charges, you want to be able to say, "You want backup? Sure thing. It'll take about forty-five minutes. Go load a hundred pages into your fax machine."

Digging through Florio's record, it wasn't easy to come up with myriad examples of his rampant hypocrisy, but I managed it. I managed it literally every day, though it did require a certain amount of artistic license.

I began each morning in my Trenton office by going through volumes of newspaper clippings, legislative records, and reams of old press releases from Governor Florio's office, until I'd found some interesting little factoid about the governor that I could pass on to the press. Rather than e-mail or fax these items, I added a personal touch by walking over to the statehouse and handing out copies to all the reporters on Press Row.

The statehouse, with its high arches and golden dome, looked impressive from a distance. But that winter, empty crack vials popped under my shoes as I walked just a block away from it. The ground floor of the Statehouse was as dreary and run-down as any bureaucratic outpost, and by the time you got upstairs to Press Row, the cluster of musty old offices where the newspaper reporters worked, it was even worse.

So it's no wonder that the journalists, who had to slog through this deteriorating part of town only to sit in a building that crumbled as they typed, started looking forward to my "Florio Quote of the Day," with its huge-headed caricature of the governor and its whimsical factoids. For instance:

New York Times, 1993:
FLORIO AIDE LEAVES AMID BOND INQUIRY.
Florio: "Sometimes money produces action."

What did the *Times'* headline and Florio's quote have to do with each other? Nothing at all. Hell, they didn't even come out in the same year. But once you've successfully defined your opponent, anything he's ever said and everything he's ever going to say will only serve to cement that definition further. This is why politicians and their handlers are always so frantic not to allow the competition to define them first.

In politics, the truth is what you say it is, especially if you say it first—and then continue to say it with dizzying repetition.

And, again, I said it every single day. After a few weeks, when Jim Goodman from the *Trenton Times* would see me coming toward his desk with my stack of papers, he always called out, "Here comes the Republican State Party again!"

I thought that was great. It meant I was having an impact. Even if the reporters didn't care for the message, they knew it was coming every day. They might file away one of my releases and reference it later or they might just trash it. All that mattered was frequency. They knew that an anti-Florio message was coming every day, at the same reliable time every day. That regularity made my messages a part of their daily process. It meant I was penetrating the press—whether they liked it or not, whether they realized it or not.

The Republicans still hadn't even picked a nominee to run against Florio, but I was starting to work as if the campaign were in full swing, putting in twelve-hour days and living on Coke and chewing tobacco. One day I felt that the strain was starting to get to me because it was the dead of winter and I couldn't cool down no matter what. I had the office door wide open, with gusts of snowy wind blowing in, my collar undone and my sleeves rolled up, yet I was still drenched in sweat. So I locked up the office early and went back to Lawrenceville, a small town thirty minutes from Trenton where I'd moved from Manhattan, to rest up.

That night, I was cooking mac and cheese in my kitchen when I got a call from the Trenton Fire Department. It turned out that the basement of my office had been in flames all day, and the entire building had been engulfed about an hour after I'd left it. I really was becoming quite the seasoned operative—I was working so hard to spin my message that I didn't even notice it when hell itself reached up from the bowels of the earth to destroy my office.

One thing I had learned from observing the Clinton/Gore campaign was that you don't ascend to the heights of political power by backing obvious winners. That may sound counterintuitive, but working in that world at the time it made a lot of sense, and especially knowing the history of James Carville. When he got the job of running the Clinton campaign, he was in his late forties with more than his fair share of losses. Then, in 1990, he picked a forty-point underdog for the U.S. Senate in Pennsylvania who went on to trounce a former U.S. attorney general who had come into the contest with every advantage. That come-from-behind win made Carville a sudden golden boy; managing Bill Clinton from a backwater to the White House made him a rock star.

You make your name by winning the race that can't be won.

So when Christie Todd Whitman was nominated in June 1993 to run against Florio, I wasn't chomping at the bit to get on her team. In the first place, I would have been positioned beneath a whole squad of other campaign staffers. Second, a Whitman victory over an increasingly unpopular incumbent wasn't going to make me stand out in my field—even in New Jersey.

The Republican assembly guys I'd made friends with while I was doing opposition research all directed me to the assembly race for District 11. There were two Republican incumbent candidates, assemblymen Steve Corodemus and Tom Smith, and their '91 victory was considered a fluke, a purely symbolic message to Florio by the district's registered Democrats that they were pissed off at his tax hike. The idea that they would actually remain in office for a second term was universally dismissed.

That was the race for me. In that race was the whole point of paying fifteen grand for GSPM's imitation parchment.

It also dovetailed well with the ridiculous five-year plan I had dreamed up in grad school: I would manage and win my first race within a year of my graduation so I could move up and run a congressional race, win that, and spend some time as a Congress member's chief of staff, run a Senate campaign, and then a presidential campaign. After all, what else is there to do before you turn thirty?

The job of campaign manager for Corodemus and Smith wasn't a difficult one to land, since nobody else seemed to want it. Besides, my "Al from Bay Head" shtick was perfect for District 11. The campaigns' headquarters were just twenty minutes north of my family's beach house and my grandmother's bay house. I even stayed with some family friends in Bay Head during the campaign.

Local or not, though, I still spent my first thirty days getting suspicious looks. Candidates don't simply accept you at face value. You have to walk through the fire together before you even know whether your candidate likes you—or whether you like him.

Corodemus was a young attorney who walked with a significant limp, which he didn't explain to me and which I didn't ask about. His running mate was Tom Smith, an old, old black man who'd been chief of police in Asbury Park during the riots in 1970, and whose reaction to those riots had been, I'd heard, to lock himself in his office. Tom Smith was a very sweet guy, just not someone you'd have wanted on the ramparts at the Alamo. I liked him, but I especially liked the idea that managing a campaign for a black Republican would further distinguish me in my profession. But, between the two assemblymen, I considered Corodemus my chief candidate due to his superior fund-raising.

This was my first campaign, my Big Shot, even if the position up for grabs was one most people would never so much as think about. The last thing I was going to be was the guy who shows up, leans back behind his desk, and, snapping his suspenders, says, "I'm the big thinker. Show me your poll numbers and I'm gonna tell you what to do."

I got in early, I stayed late. I returned all my calls. If Corodemus gave me a list of things to do, I didn't go home until I had completed every one of them.

Ninety percent of any campaign is in the details, the niggling tasks—the breaking of your back. That labor is also the only way you can really earn anyone's respect. There are a hundred ways to earn owed favors, paybacks, and kickbacks, but none of those is equivalent to respect. Respect is the gold standard.

I don't know if I won Corodemus's respect in that first month—every one of the behind-the-scenes operatives in either party believes that he or she has earned the respect of colleagues; most of them are woefully misinformed—but I know I did everything I could to earn it.

Our opponents were Daniel Jacobson and John Villapiano. Villapiano was something of a local legend whose brother had played for the Oakland Raiders. He was a nice enough guy—even ran a summer camp right on the Jersey Shore. It wasn't until the fall that things started getting really nasty.

My salary was being paid through the Assembly Republican Majority campaign committee, which was run by Assembly Speaker "Chuck" Garabed Haytaian in Trenton, rather than by the Corodemus campaign itself. So there were always lingering questions in Corodemus's mind as to whom I was actually working for—him, or the Party apparatus in Trenton. The awkward arrangement was complicated further by the fact that Corodemus had no prior approval over what kind of campaign ads the assembly's campaign committee would run on his behalf. The committee never even showed him the pieces before they ran, though they did show me. So I knew what was coming, my candidate didn't, and I couldn't tell him.

Through the campaign committee, I ended up working closely with Dave Sackett, of the prominent Republican polling firm the Tarrance Group, and the GOP direct mail vendor of the moment, David Welch. Right at the beginning Sackett told me, "To win this race, you've just got to annihilate the other guys. This is not about your guys and what they've done. It's about the other guys being bad, tax-crazy, warrior Democrats."

So I knew what we had in store for the Dems come fall, I knew that it would be ugly, and then uglier and uglier. And I could not have been happier. The gunslinger-mercenary aspect of my personality pricked up at the thought of finally getting into a fight after all that battle training in grad school. My training had armed me with a vast array of aggressive, win-at-all-costs techniques, and I felt like a soldier who had been issued the world's perfect rifle but still hadn't had the chance to get a round off in combat. I wanted to pick a fight, have a fight, and win a fight. In fact, that part of me felt that things weren't going to get quite ugly *enough*. So I fixed that problem in September, when I attended an editorial board meeting of the *Asbury Park Press*.

Having all the candidates in an election show up to make their case to a paper's editors and reporters is an ancient ritual that is supposed to help the paper decide whom to back in a coming election. For the most part, the process is completely vestigial, since the paper has already decided whom it will support based solely on party lines. The whole affair was pretty much tame and polite, until the very end, when everybody was standing from their chairs to leave and I managed to get up and lean over Jacobson.

"I'm going to destroy you," I said, just loud enough so that only he could hear it. "Your career is over."

Jacobson looked at me with a combination of disbelief and confusion, and I moved past him rather than giving him a chance to respond. I knew what we had in store for him and Villapiano, our opponents, and the adolescent in me just couldn't help but to stick out his jaw and dare them to take a swing at it. It was coming and they couldn't do a thing about it: I was going to win my first race.

One of the first pieces of Sackett-tested, Welch-designed direct mail we sent out that fall was made to look like a pink slip. It accused Villapiano of orchestrating massive layoffs at his summer camp while at the same time giving himself a huge bonus.

And it was absolutely true. Of course, the workers he had fired were camp counselors whose jobs had expired with the summer. His "bonus" was what he had paid himself at the end of the summer after he had settled all of his business's accounts for the year. It was actually a very honorable way to conduct business, but as far as the voters were concerned, he was a scumbag who had just fired fifty people while paying a huge dividend to himself.

Sure, Villapiano explained his actions to the press, and pointed out that we had taken a perfectly innocent truth and twisted it.

No one listened.

We had painted him and nothing he could say would change that.

Our next mailings linked Villapiano and Jacobson to rotten real estate deals in Camden County that had nothing whatsoever to do with either of them. It had everything to do with the governor's office, but since those deals were ratified through the legislative process before Villapiano was tossed out of the assembly for his support of the Florio tax hike, we could say, "He voted for it! Look at this sweetheart deal he gave to this guy over here who returned the favor with buckets of campaign cash."

Villapiano and Jacobson had, in fact, no decision-making power at all in those sweetheart deals, and yet we smeared them as Trenton insiders who fired people, screwed you out of your money, and gave kickback deals to people who donated to their campaign.

Was Steve Corodemus on board with this? God no! Every time a new piece of direct mail came out, he would tell me, "You've got to fucking stop this direct mail, Al! I *live* here! People are coming up to me and cursing in my face!"

"No sweat," I always told him, "I'll stop the mail." I had, obviously, no intention of stopping the mail. I wouldn't even make a single phone call about it. I saw my job as being a firewall between Trenton and Corodemus because the annihilation tactics that Steve so hated were the only way he could win.

A candidate's best intentions can lose them the election. They rarely understand that. They live inside their own heads, where things are black and white. Elections are not won inside one person's set of standards. It takes a wider, crummier view of things.

And so the hits just kept on coming.

What could possibly go wrong?

In late October, two weeks before Election Day, Corodemus, Tom Smith, and I showed up for a debate in a high school auditorium in Wall, New Jersey. No voter really gives a crap about a state assembly debate, so it was just the four candidates, some campaign staffers, and a reporter from the *Asbury Park Press*. I sat through the usual talking points for about an hour and, just as the debate was coming to an end, Jacobson stood up and said, "Steve Corodemus, have you ever been mentioned in a court filing regarding domestic violence?"

Steve's face went blank. "I, uh—I, I don't know what you're talking about."

"Are you sure," Jacobson pushed on, "that you've never been charged with this state statute in any kind of court proceeding?" He then read off the statute number for mis52

demeanor domestic violence.

Again Steve said he didn't know what Jacobson was talking about. Then everything blew right the hell up.

"Well, you know," Jacobson said, "court records indicate allegations that you beat your wife and that you're a deadbeat dad."

It was all a blur after that. The only thing I remember is old Tom Smith croaking "That's a bunch of poppycock" and then immediately vaporizing from the auditorium. He hauled ass so fast that all that was left of him were some squiggly phosphorescent lines. We never saw him again for the last two weeks of the race. Tom, the trusty running mate, was in the bunker and Steve was on his own.

I hustled Steve out of the building and into his car. He insisted on driving—he had a big gold Crown Victoria. We were heading down Route 138 in total silence. It was up to Steve to break that silence; I couldn't do it for him. What was I going to say? "Hey, Steve, did you beat your wife?"

When we came to the entrance to the Garden State Parkway, Steve had to choose between making a left or a right, and he just couldn't do it. He just kept staring zombie-eyed at the fork in the road as we closed in on it. In the end he just slowed down until his bumper tapped the guardrail.

For another minute we just sat there.

"I threw the keys at her," he finally said. "I was angry. But they didn't hit her."

"That's fine, Steve," I said. "Let's just go."

Looking back, I don't think he even realized that we were in a car, or that I was there at all. It was like his life was over and he was talking to himself.

"We hit them too hard," Steve said.

"Yeah," I said, "those direct mail guys are just out of control."

Steve was devastated—he was also wrong. In any campaign, but especially the little ones that don't get any press, all anyone hears and remembers are the negatives. People are busy, and in the midst of their busy lives they're also inundated by media. As a campaign manager, you've got to cut through all that incessant buzzing—not just the crime stories, the coupons, the comic strips, but also CNN, Howard Stern, Bill O'Reilly, and whatever fashion show is parading on the local nightly news. Are you going to accomplish that with happy little butterfly stories?

It's a sweet idea, if you never want to get anyone elected.

We wound up in a diner around midnight. Steve was crushed but I felt like I had just hit the mother lode. Here I am on my first campaign and I get to do extreme crisis control. It's the dream scenario: we're leading in the polls, two weeks away from the election, and we've just been hit with a major threat to our victory. What do we do?

This was what I had trained for. I was wide awake and I started shooting questions at Steve.

"What's your ex-wife going to say? Will she back you up on this wife-beating charge? Will she say that it never happened?"

"I think so."

"And the deadbeat dad stuff?"

"My son . . . Everyone should have the life my son's had."

He filled me in a little. His son, Dimitrios, was in his first year of college and Steve had never missed a support payment. This was all news to me. I was pumped up to get to work on this thing, but I needed more facts first.

"Where are your ex-wife and son at?"

Suddenly, Steve said to me, "Do you know why I walk with a limp?"

"No, Steve—but let's get back to you beating up your wife."

Here I was reminded that Steve Corodemus was a defense attorney, and that he viewed the election as a jury trial.

"Let me tell you what happened to me," he said. "I was working in New York on Valentine's Day. I'd bought some flowers for my wife. So I was heading home with these flowers and I was standing on the platform waiting for the train. . . ."

He told me that when the express came through, its force sucked him up against it and then bounced him down onto the tracks.

"So there I am, lying on the train tracks, bleeding, and the only thing I can think of is, Hold on to these flowers; I've got to get these flowers to my wife."

It was a good story, but not quite what we needed at the moment. I figured I would file it away for later. In the meantime, I knew I'd gotten all I could out of Steve for the night. I suggested that he go home and get some rest. He was going to need it.

The first thing I saw in the office the next morning was the front page of the *Asbury Park Press*. All the allegations were there. After consulting with Steve, I decided we would tackle the deadbeat dad issue first, since his relationship with his son wasn't nearly as tricky as his relationship with his ex-wife. Dimitrios agreed to do a radio spot that we'd plaster across the district the next morning, which was the earliest that we could do a good media buy. I booked 1010 WINS, WFAN, anything a commuter from the 11th District might listen to on the way to work.

Dimitrios's message was straightforward: "My dad has always supported us, even through the tough times. And he always takes time for family events—going to ball games, helping me with homework, and just being a great dad. He even pays my college tuition." And then the righteous anger: "You should be ashamed of yourself, and quit lying about us, Mr. Villapiano. In other words, leave my family alone!"

There would be nothing straightforward in negotiating with the ex.

I wrote out a list of things for Steve to ask her to consider doing for him. He consulted with me again after getting off the phone with her. The results were not promising.

"Will she do a radio spot?" I asked.

"No."

"Will she do a press conference?"

"No."

"Will she at least denounce the wife-beating charge?"

The problem was that that accusation had been made in a court proceeding. She couldn't just come around now and say she had lied under oath.

"Well, fuck," I said. "What *will* she do?"

"She wants to have a conversation," he said. "Come on, we're going to her office."

So it was back into the Crown Vic again. When we rolled up in front of her office he told me to wait in the car. A minute later I could see the both of them, Steve and his ex, through a big bay window.

I guess I have a twisted voyeur side to me. It wasn't enough just to watch them through the window, I actually called some buddies from the assembly campaign committee headquarters on the car phone and started giving them a play-by-play.

"He's sitting down. Oh, he just got up, he's pacing. He's looking sheepish. Oh, she's not looking happy."

As it turned out, while I was watching them, she was rolling him. I couldn't hear it, but you could just see that he was getting his ass kicked.

It was such a surreal thing. I was a twenty-five-year-old guy without a care in the world and now I was in the middle of this man's life while it could be coming apart. It was much more exposure to his inner world than I ever wanted. After forty-five minutes, he came back to the car deflated, just sapped. It looked to me as if he'd just run a hundred miles across a desert.

"Well," he said, "she will denounce the accusation."

"Great! That's great!"

"Yes. And I just had to extend her alimony. It was about to expire."

I was amazed. He was a good guy—kind, decent—and she basically put a gun to his head.

I drafted a denial statement for her that afternoon and sent it to her office. After a few edits, she finally signed it and we released it to the press. One day after the attack and we were fighting back.

"Nothing could be further from the truth," it read. "I really don't care who wins this election. But if it matters to any voters, let them be influenced by the truth rather than baseless political rhetoric." In case the Dems didn't get the point, the release further stated, "Fair is fair, and the truth shouldn't be distorted for political gain," which is kind of hard to argue with, coming from the original source of the accusations. The enemy had to back up.

So we had the son and the mother taken care of, but I felt we still needed a little something extra to make it perfect. In order to get full value out of that attack on us, we had to make it look like the last-ditch effort of desperate men. For that to happen, we needed something to make Steve seem . . . empathetic.

The main reporter on the race was Lisa Kruse from the *Asbury Park Press,* and she hated us. She wasn't buying anything we said—never had, never would. As far as she was concerned, the wife-beater, deadbeat dad stuff was proper comeuppance for our trail of sleazy campaigning. And she was pretty much the only reporter who could give us what we needed.

We were discussing how we might win her over when Steve said, "The funny thing is, I just received this letter." He went to his breast pocket and pulled out a letter. I remember checking the post-mark and seeing that it actually was recent. The letter had been writ-ten by a friend of Dimitrios's, a black kid from a single-mother household, who had written Steve from college to thank him for having been like a surrogate father to him.

"That's fucking great!" I said. "I've got to make a copy of this."

About half an hour later, I put a copy of the letter in Lisa Kruse's hands.

"You see?" I told her. "He's not a monster. Just look at this let-ter." Again, she wasn't buying it. Fine. I made a decision. "Okay," I told her. "I can bring you this kid!"

A day later, we flew him up from Georgia, or someplace. I never knew his name. He may have told me when I picked him up at the airport, but it has long left my memory. Quite frankly, it didn't mat-ter. What mattered to me was that he was from a single-mother home, he was black, he considered Steve Corodemus a surrogate dad, and he was there to help in a time of dire need. That's all I needed to know.

From the airport we drove straight to the *Asbury Park Press*, and we met Lisa Kruse in the lobby.

"It's very nice to meet you," she told him. Then she took me aside. "I don't want you here."

It was a huge roll of the dice, leaving the kid alone with her. Who knew what he would say? But she wouldn't talk to him if I had stayed there, and it would have looked like a total snow job if I'd taken him away without letting her speak to him, so there really wasn't any choice but to gamble.

I waited outside. Kruse brought him out forty-five minutes later. She never did mention him again, but the tone of her articles changed after that meeting. Steve Corodemus wasn't just a politi-cian in her writing anymore. Her language softened. We had made it too hard for her to keep writing bad things about Steve after meet-ing this kid. How could she? We had turned a corner, and we had done it in five days.

It was about knowing what buttons to push and when to push them.

We won by 5,000 votes. Steve Corodemus went on to serve sixteen years in the state legislature. Tom Smith died in office in 2002.

As for me, I had made my bones and was ready to go to Washington. At least, *I* thought so.

FOUR

*B*ill Clinton had started laying the groundwork for the Republican Revolution of 1994—as well as my own rise in the Republican power ranks—almost as soon as he took office in '93, with an income tax increase that struck us GOP folks as morally outrageous, considering that we had most of the country's money. In the House of Representatives, the deciding vote in favor of the Clinton budget had been cast by Democrat Marjorie Margolies-Mezvinsky of Pennsylvania's 13th Congressional District. The Republicans on the House floor literally chanted "Bye-bye Margie!" when she cast it.

I was going to have the honor of heading to Pennsylvania to unseat her.

Well, that was the idea, anyway.

Ellen Harley, a Republican state representative from Montgomery County, Pennsylvania, was the only announced Republican candidate vying for Margolies-Mezvinsky's seat when I took the job of managing her House campaign. Bill Ulrey, who had hired me at the New Jersey Republican State Committee a year earlier, had recommended me for the position and I jumped at it.

We were just five months away from the May primary, and as I understood it from Ellen Harley and Ulrey, she was prepared to raise and spend $750,000 to win. Beating Margolies-Mezvinsky was the brass ring in 1994 and Margolies-Mezvinsky was a guaranteed loser. Pennsylvania's 13th Congressional District at the time was two-to-one Republican. Margolies-Mezvinsky was a Democrat in a wealthy Philly suburb where everybody else was a Republican and she had just voted to allow Bill Clinton to pick their pockets. Whichever Republican faced her in the fall general election was a shoo-in. This race would be like dynamiting fish in a barrel.

For my career this was like being called up from Double-A ball to pitch in the bigs, and I knew I was ready.

Ellen Harley's base of Montgomery County was better known as the Main Line. Harley looked as if she had mainlined the Main Line, right down to the perfect hair and manicure, and the spacious home north of Philadelphia. High-profile campaigns don't offer themselves up every day, so I probably would have worked for any of the primary contenders, but I genuinely liked Ellen as a candidate. Aside from presenting well, Ellen was politically experienced, pragmatic, and had an aggressive taste for the jugular. Most importantly, though, she was offering me the job.

She also had her weaknesses. Most obvious was the fact that she was a fanatically pro-choice Republican. Another was the fact that she had briefly entered the Republican primary for the U.S. Senate nomination but quickly dropped out when it became clear she couldn't win. So now her campaign for the House primary had a handicap from the get-go, the perception that she was trying to cherry-pick for any higher office she could get.

What she had going for her was that the Republican good-old-boy network was in chaos. The candidate they wanted, a silver-maned pro-choice state senator by the name of Stewart "Stu" Greenleaf, was waffling. He had dipped a toe in the water and then scampered to the warmth and comfort of his state senate seat—it was never clear why. The other contender was an overweight, mustachioed backslapper named Jon Fox. Fox had had the distinction of getting his ass handed to him by Margolies-Mezvinsky two years earlier, and so the boys in the smoky back room had their doubts about his ability to win. What I didn't know at the time, unfortunately, was that the Party infrastructure in Pennsylvania was fractured along ultraconservative versus progressive-conservative lines, and that Ellen's faction was on the wrong side of the schism. Ulrey was a high-level New Jersey Party guy, so when he referred me to Ellen I had assumed she was on good terms with the machine. What Ulrey hadn't mentioned was that he knew Ellen through personal, not political, channels, and that she had won her state legislature seat by running against the Party apparatus in 1990.

So, knowing as little as I did, I sensed that Harley was the best bet. If the fellas at Party headquarters were willing to back a pro-choicer like Greenleaf, then they were willing to stomach Harley, too, right? My other wager was that they wouldn't risk Fox taking another beating at the polls.

Many such misapprehensions were revealed to me when the Party threw its weight behind Fox a few weeks after I had signed on with Ellen. Still, I liked that she was willing to put it on the line against the bosses. To me that was the true Republican spirit free will, free market, free enterprise. Besides, I'd been raised by a single mother, so assertive women were the norm in my life.

Even if I was going against the GOP elite in Pennsylvania, none of my Party guys in New Jersey cared about that, and Jersey was my base. In Philly I was just a carpetbagger; I didn't have any close ties there. My attitude was that the real horse race was the general election, and that I needed a horse, any horse, to ride in it. Hell, I'd have settled for a mule. When I wasn't working I was back in Trenton and Princeton barhopping with Pat Torpey and other GOP campaign operatives. New Jersey pols in leadership positions were referring me to jobs—they had my real allegiance.

As for the Harley campaign, I figured that if Ellen would just let me do my thing we could squeeze by in the primary and then bludgeon our opponent for a victory over the Dems in the general election. A pro-choice Republican can do great things in a general election, but who do you suppose are the majority of registered Republicans that bother turning out for a primary? It's the Jesus-loves-guns crowd every time. I watched it again and again for ten years straight. Some stereotypes didn't just land here from outer space. So we were in for a hell of a fight. The fact that Ellen was promoting herself as "socially tolerant" wasn't going to be any help. The mouth-breathers who decide GOP primaries might allow people who steal their money and send their children to impossible wars to get away with anything, but they'll cut no such slack for baby-killers.

As it turned out, though, Ellen's worst enemies were not the right-wing goons or the old-time Party hacks, but her own endless circle of friends. Imagine a few dozen rich suburban sorority girls who had reached middle age without a single job between them suddenly deciding to put their pal into Congress.

By the time I showed up, they had already spent a ton of money on ridiculously lavish offices in King of Prussia, a northwest suburb of Philadelphia. Every campaign headquarters I'd worked out of was either a run-down little cubbyhole or the candidate's own business office, and here they'd set themselves up with luxury accommodations in a top-of-the-line shopping mall. And there was no organization to speak of, not even any staff, just a lot of moneyed housewives and long-ago debuted debutantes gabbing on the phones and making lunch dates.

The ladies did have their ideas about finding staffers, though. After all, they had plenty of sons and daughters who had to get into politics as soon as possible. I had barely started when Ellen had me interview one of them for a job. I didn't object. We would need warm bodies to run errands and work the phones.

In walked a good-looking young guy, and he was blind. Now, as anyone who's worked a campaign knows, at least half of the things you say to your campaign workers begin with the words "Get in the car and go to . . ." As for working the phones, well, if a political campaign was a long-term affair, he could have been accommodated, but it's the exact opposite of that; it's get in, get out, and make as big of a mess as you have to in between. At end of day, I had to tell the kid that his skill set didn't fit the campaign's needs.

That was great. Not only were Ellen's jobless gal pals getting in my way and spending my budget, they had also just caused me the only crisis of conscience of my political career. It was a short crisis, to be sure; he wouldn't have gotten the interview in the first place without his mother's inside pull and it was the right decision to let him go, but I did feel for the kid all the same.

The next executive decision I made on that campaign was pretty much my last. I cut our budget by getting rid of the shopping mall salon. Ellen simply wasn't raising enough money to pay for it. Instead I found an old dentist's office. The heat wasn't great for a winter campaign, but the price was right, and it came with a huge, lighted parking lot. Ellen and her gang hated the place but I thought it was the coolest thing. A big swivel-arm dental lamp had been left behind and I used it as my desk lamp.

That, effectively, was the end of my management. I went from being Ellen's campaign manager to being its spokesman in a matter of weeks because I just couldn't hold off all the Friends of Harley who were trampling all over the camp. They were very wealthy, very strong-willed women who thought they knew how to run a campaign. Essentially, Ellen was one of them.

The main problem was that they couldn't seem to see that the wealth that had cushioned them from life's blows was proving a real stumbling block for the campaign. The difference between their fiscal reality and that of most voters was completely lost on Ellen and her set. One day my Passat got cut in half in a run-in with a city bus and when I went to buy a new one the next day, the only car left on the VW lot was a purple Jetta. So I drove my new Jetta back to campaign headquarters to take Ellen to an event and when she took one look at the car, she told me, "I'm not riding in that thing."

"Why the hell not?"

"It's purple. I'm not riding in that purple Barney car."

Fifteen minutes later, a friend of Ellen's picked her up in a Jaguar.

Her reasons for running may have been well intentioned, but she was a woman who had always had the means to have everything her own way, and the bottom line was that her way wasn't based in political reality.

When her friends wanted to take over fund-raising, Ellen let them. She thought wealth would attract wealth. But again political reality intervened. The only issue her friends wanted to sell was pro-choice. They were going to get a pro-choice Republican into Congress and that was that. They brought in a consultant straight out of the Republican pro-choice movement and then they refused to raise money from any source outside of that wing of the Party. Unsurprisingly, the money dried up.

I had been begging Ellen every day to back away from the liberal stuff for the primary. Now that was going to be impossible, since every disclosure report from the Federal Election Commission (FEC) would make it obvious that all our money was coming from pro-choice donors. With the Party backing Fox, Ellen's only advantage was her wealthy girlfriends and all the money they could raise through their social networks.

Except that they couldn't. There wasn't any money. Ellen and her people thought they could beat Fox by buying up a lot of TV spots in relatively liberal Philadelphia. But when the time came, they couldn't afford the ads. So much for the promise of a $750,000 budget that had helped lure me into the campaign.

When Ellen realized that she was running out of money, she began showing a personality trait that just did not work for her. Where previously she'd been aggressively confident, now she was becoming aggressively shrill. With the Party opposing her and her friends encouraging her every whim, the campaign swerved further and further away from addressing the basic facts of a Republican primary.

For my part, I was trying to focus on anything that didn't involve abortion. Back then, the Philadelphia Phillies had a relief pitcher named Mitch Williams, aka "Wild Thing." He had blown the World Series that fall by throwing a home run pitch in Game Six. So I started calling Fox "the Mitch Williams of the Pennsylvania Republican Party" because he was the guy who'd lost the fort to Margolies-Mezvinsky in '92. Frankly, it hadn't been his fault. Bill Clinton had overrun George Bush that year and Fox just happened to be Johnny-on-the-spot. In any case, the nickname didn't stick.

Because I lacked funds for a solid TV ad buy, my main weapons became direct mail and the press release. Even our direct mail vendor, Dave Murray, whom I'd brought in from New Jersey, had lost all faith in the campaign. "What are you doing with her?" he once asked me. "She's not going to win. And she's crazy!"

I knew we were just running out the clock, but I had made a commitment to stick with the campaign through Election Day, so there I was, sticking with it.

Fox had once written a friendly sentencing-letter for a convicted drug trafficker, attesting to the dealer's character, so I sent out a direct mail piece that read, "Ellen Harley wrote a bill to make criminals serve their prison terms. No more early parole. No more softhearted parole boards. Jon Fox wrote a letter of recommendation for a man convicted of selling 300 pounds of cocaine." I just wanted to make her look hardfisted somewhere, anywhere. It wasn't enough.

In Ellen's defense, there was definitely a sexist element in the way that the Party was treating her. The string-pullers at the county level had been left with a bad taste in their mouths when a woman had beaten Fox in '92. And now, damn it, he was still their boy and they weren't about to have another woman come along and upset the natural order that they meant to impose.

Rather than have a spirited, democratic debate on the matter, they expected Ellen to shut her mouth and step aside. Fox quite literally would not debate her. I made an issue of that fact by calling a press conference and having Ellen sit in a chair opposite a duck-hunting decoy.

When Fox was reached for comment, the fat, white good old boy told the reporter, "Where is she? I'll mud-wrestle her!"

We tried to use that comment in a campaign aimed at women voters, pointing out that Fox was a chauvinist pig, but you can't win a Republican primary with women voters, at least not the kind who can see what was offensive about the remark.

Ellen decided that her last chance at the nomination would be to grab it at the Republican county convention. It was a terrible idea. The winner of a Republican convention is almost always dictated by the county machine, and the machine had picked Fox. So Ellen had no chance of convincing the delegates to vote her way. As slim as it was, her only real chance to win the nomination was to focus all her energy and resources on the Republican primary election. Just because the GOP delegates would vote for Fox as ordered at the convention, it didn't necessarily mean that everyday Republican voters would follow suit in the primary. If Ellen skipped the convention altogether, she could then go on to woo primary voters on the platform that she wasn't just another cog in the Party machine. But if she entered the convention, she wouldn't be able to play the outsider card when the primary rolled around. So, yes, the primary was a long shot—but it was the only shot she had.

"If you run in the convention and lose," I told her, "you'll have to come up with some rationale for staying in the race after that."

As usual, she had to have it her way. She was a Republican state representative. A lot of delegates and power players had personally promised to support her. They didn't. At the convention, Fox made his speech, Ellen made her speech, and she lost just as I had predicted.

Etiquette and tradition dictate that if you compete in and don't win the convention you pledge your support to the winner, then step down and wait for next time.

So it went that on a frigid day in March, at a typical Main Line country club, Ellen Harley came face-to-face with reality. The convention delegates had rejected her, and me, too, as far as I was concerned. Ellen had bet all her political aspirations on one panicked roll of the dice at that convention. By asking for the convention endorsement, she was also tacitly accepting the dynamic that what the delegates did was binding. If she had won she would have insisted that Jon Fox, and anybody else, drop out of the race and support her candidacy.

But when she lost, there was only one thing to do: condemn the process as the antiquated remnants of the good-old-boy network, reject the judgment of the delegates, spurn the Party, and press on, full speed ahead. Everybody else could go to hell.

You can't ask people for their vote at the convention and then pretend it doesn't mean anything. If you do, you're saying "Your vote is meaningless to me." For most people, their vote is the only thing they've ever had.

Dismally, Harley did in fact stay in the race right through to the primary election, at which point we got our teeth kicked in. By then she had earned it. In her hotel suite, with a hundred supporters downstairs taking in the returns on television and hitting the cash bar heavily to drown their disappointment, I said, "Ellen, it's over. There are a hundred people downstairs and you need to concede. Unify the Party."

"Okay," she said, "let's go." We got in the elevator. All the Philadelphia press was there waiting for her. She stepped to the mic on the dais and, in true Ellen fashion, said, "Ladies and gentlemen, the fat lady hasn't sung!"

Then she marched off the stage.

She may as well have kicked me in the chest. I hustled off the stage and tried to sneak out unobserved, but it was a scrum of reporters.

"Mr. Raymond, what did Harley mean?"

"Are you challenging the results?"

"It's over. My sincere congratulations to Jon Fox and his supporters," I told them, and got the hell away from there.

After Fox had won the convention, one Republican source told the *Philadelphia Daily News,* "Don't forget, this is a party run by boys. Fox was nominated because they can control him more than they can control her." Ellen and I were on escalators moving in opposite directions. The people who had supported her getting into politics on the state level had decided she wasn't worthy to serve at the national level. The Party she'd belonged to for all those years didn't even want her as a member unless she behaved exactly as it told her to behave. In fact, the Party wouldn't so much as discuss the possibility of her choosing her own career trajectory. At that point, I would not have believed anyone who told me that Party loyalty is ultimately a one-way street. I would have said they were crazy. Yet I had just watched it happen to Ellen Harley. Still, somehow I thought it was Ellen Harley who was crazy.

It was my first lesson in intraparty politics. I believed that Ellen had had as much claim to the nomination as anyone else, but what I took away was that it's all but futile to work against the machine. My attitude was, why work against it when you can work with it? It was so much easier, and the pay was probably better. Ellen was finished with the Party and I was becoming more enamored, more deeply indoctrinated every day. It contained all my social circles, all the people who gave me work. The Party was becoming my whole life.

Almost.

I'd been going out with the same girl, Elizabeth, since college. Elizabeth was in graduate school for art history and she couldn't stand it when I brought her along to Party events where she had to socialize with the rank and file of New Jersey Republican politics. Just after the Harley campaign, I took her to a fund-raiser in my old stomping ground of Sussex County, at the home of the New Jersey Republican Party chair, Ginnie Littell. In character, humor, and attitude, Ginnie was the exception to the Republican rule, but her guests were not. Whenever one of them would ask Elizabeth what she did for a living, Elizabeth—in her motorcycle jacket, matching boots, and a babydoll sundress—would tell them, "I'm a socialist."

Finally, I took her aside and said, "Jesus, Lizzie, what the hell are you doing?"

"Oh, relax," she said. "These people are jackasses!"

"That may be," I said, "but they're *my* jackasses!"

FIVE

*E*llen Harley ended up packing her whole house and running away down south after losing the 1994 primary. It turned out to be a great opportunity for me. While the Party considered it something of a foregone conclusion that Jon Fox would go on to defeat Marjorie Margolies-Mezvinsky, it was raining money on a congressional race in New Jersey that would take a miracle for the Republicans to win.

I wasn't much for miracles, but I had learned a few good dirty tricks, and I figured they'd do just as well in a pinch.

The Harley primary loss and, to an extent, the Corodemus New Jersey assembly victory, had taught me that the worst kind of client you can have is one who holds too firmly to his or her ideals. Left unchecked, the same moral inspiration that may initially win a candidate a groundswell of support will end up wasting the time and effort of supporters, since it will inevitably lose him or her the election. Ellen Harley sacrificed any chance she had at winning the primary by beating the pro-choice drum instead of doing what was necessary to raise funds, and if Corodemus had had his way, he would never have allowed me to savage his opponent on the campaign trail. Causes are all well and good, but what good can you do them if you can't get elected? And getting elected takes a more, well, subtle set of ethics than rallying a cause.

Bill Martini, whose campaign I ran for New Jersey's 8th Congressional District in 1994, was not encumbered by any such ideals. Martini didn't even have what you could properly call a platform. However, he did boast a million-dollar budget and the full enthusiasm of the burgeoning Republican Revolution—the Southern-based neoconservative movement that was using Clinton's tax hike, and the illusion that Republicans were somehow more oriented toward "family values" than the Democrats, in an attempt to take over both the Senate and the House of Representatives in the 1994 midterm elections.

Martini's was the second-most expensive congressional race in the country that year. It was so crucial to the GOP's planned takeover of the legislature that Newt Gingrich himself came and stumped for us and gave us a check for the cause. Every congressional race that could unseat a Democratic incumbent and help put a Republican in the Speaker's chair was important that year, but if we could elect Martini we'd be snatching away historically Democratic territory—and the Dems would have to spend a terrific amount of money if they were ever going to get it back. Lofty platforms such as Gingrich's Contract with America didn't mean a thing in a local street fight like the one we were engaged in, but Gingrich's presence sent the message to everyone—from the voters to the national media—that this was a race that mattered.

Martini's fist-through-the-drywall managerial approach had already burned through five campaign managers when he hired me that May before the election. The staffers had a pool going as to how long I would last, none of them placing bets on anything beyond three weeks. Martini had been a state prosecutor in Hudson County for a few years, an assistant U.S. attorney after that, and a defense attorney for sixteen more, and had the easy temperament you'd expect of such a man. Still, I thought he was the perfect candidate for me.

I was twenty-six at the time, had just fought and lost my first federal campaign, and would have taken pretty much anything that came along, but what Martini offered was a career-making challenge. The only elective offices he had ever held were that of city councilman and county freeholder—which is New Jersey's equivalent of a county legislator—yet here he was challenging an incumbent Democrat for a House seat in one of the staunchest Democratic strongholds in the country. Any operative who could pull that off could write his own ticket afterward.

While Martini's county-elected position was rather small-fry stuff, it also meant that he had already cleared one of his major hurdles: the inevitable ethics attacks. His opponent, freshman representative Herb Klein, had already gone after Martini for having defended some particularly grisly murderers, rapists, and tax cheats in his private practice. But that tactic didn't gain Klein any real leverage, because it was like denouncing a garbage man for touching garbage all day: Martini's response was more or less "Hey, that's my fucking job." So I knew that Klein would be digging for better dirt. My first order of business was to find it before he did.

The candidate vulnerability study is a highly recommended yet underutilized tactic for understanding a candidate's potential weaknesses before the opponent can have a field day with them. It's a tricky business; you're basically sitting your boss down and asking him if he's ever driven drunk, used cocaine, or cheated on his taxes. What the hell can he say? Of course, I couldn't have cared less how Martini spent his leisure time. The crucial question was how he spent his money—and from whence it came.

I held this all-important sit-down at Martini's private law office, which was the real campaign headquarters, not the downtown storefront where we corralled the volunteers. The storefront office was essentially a filter for the kooks—the knuckle-draggers, the gunnies, and the committed-ideologue nuts. No offense to the true believers, but it's hard to get any serious business done with someone from the God Squad twisting your ear about the evils of stem cell research while an NRA lifer demands your assurance that the black helicopters won't be swooping down to deprive him of his twin-mounted .50-caliber Brownings.

As soon as I started tossing Martini the hard questions, I could see that the former defense counselor was entirely in his element.

"Okay," I told him. "We know they're looking for something to nail you with. What are they gonna find? What do you have in your background that we should prepare for?"

He didn't squirm or show the slightest discomfort. At five eight and a fit 190 pounds, he had a football player's frame and a gunslinger's gait. Leaning forward across his enormous desk, he folded his hands beneath his chin, his lips pulling back from his teeth in a confidential grin.

"Some of the guys I've taken money from," he said, "they might have kind of a . . . you know, a *questionable* background."

"Questionable how?" I asked. "What kind of questions are we talking about?"

He didn't offer a direct answer, but started going through papers on his desk, licking his fingers while shuffling documents. That was just his usual mode—constant motion.

"One particular contributor," he began again offhandedly while reading over some notes, "is a contractor named Larry Tromeur."

Tromeur had been the chief architect on the badly—some said corruptly—mismanaged construction of a Passaic County administration building that ended up costing taxpayers more than $25 million in overruns. All I needed to hear was "contractor" and "contributor" to understand the shitstorm we were about to get caught in. The very backbone of Klein's campaign against Martini was that he'd been on the freeholder board when it approved the cost overruns for the project. If Klein didn't already know that Martini had accepted a contribution from the man at the heart of the controversy, the next round of FEC financial disclosure reports would reveal it. Either way, Klein's people would use the info when it counted most—that is, just before Election Day.

In an instant, the gist of Klein's attacks would upshift from hinting at poor fiscal oversight to accusations of straight-up graft.

"So what do we do about this?" I said. "Do we give the money back?"

"What–no!" Martini seemed personally offended at the idea. "You don't give money *back*. Besides, that would only justify Klein to say that I was wrong in accepting it in the first place."

The prospect of losing the election over a lousy $1,400 donation illustrated a hugely boneheaded move on Martini's part, but there was no profit in pointing that out. Martini was quick to make that argument himself:

"It's like with this O. J. Simpson business," he said. "Bad things happen, people make mistakes–no one knows why. But why doesn't matter, am I right? What matters is what you do about it once you're faced with that mistake."

"So here we are facing it. What do we do?"

The conversation groaned on for an hour. These little one-on-one chats were often so grueling that I came to refer to them as "feeding the beast." At the end of it, I blurted out the solution as if suddenly inspired by a last-ditch vision of finally getting the hell out of that office.

"Have Tromeur throw a little money Klein's way," I said. For once, Martini stopped talking and fussing with his papers. I explained, "Tell him to make a donation to Klein's campaign big enough to make it onto the FEC report, but small enough so that his people won't even notice it. Say, two hundred and fifty dollars."

As a hired gun, I found my plan uniquely gratifying in several ways. On the one hand, it would immediately neutralize Klein's ham-fisted strike at my candidate. But the real thrill it gave me was in its utter gamesmanship. The periodic financial disclosure reports that the FEC demanded during an election had come about as a direct response to Watergate. The very existence of these filings was intended to force some level of fiscal transparency upon political campaigns. Using such a do-gooder apparatus to bend the facts beyond recognition was just plain poetry to me.

That gunslinger's smile waxed across Martini's face again. He reached across the desk, grabbed my shoulder, and said, "Now you're thinking like an attorney! Write the press release and I'll handle Tromeur."

I'm sure I looked surprised. It was so easy I could tell he had already reached the same conclusion. Maybe he had already had Tromeur write the check. I was about to ask him why we'd just gone through this prolonged exercise when his laughter cut me off.

"There's always more than one way to look at a problem. How you look at a problem dictates how you solve it. Am I right?" he said. "It takes practice, but it's a habit worth adopting. Take a good look around after you learn to see the world in a different dimension, then tell me what you see."

The world looked expansive. I was truly beginning to understand how few metaphysical limitations a person is up against once he decides that the truth is what he makes it. From then on, two plus two would equal whatever sum I found most useful.

I spent that summer working eighteen-hour days seven days a week, once again living on chewing tobacco and Coke, all the while giddily anticipating Klein's attack. Martini passed those months talking to any crowd that would listen about lower taxes and less spending, tax-and-spend liberals, all the usual fodder. It didn't matter. Whatever you talk about before Labor Day is just for the press. The messages you pay for are what count, and you don't spend a dime on advertising during the no-news cycle of the summer. My main concern during that time was keeping Martini out of the office and out of my hair for as much of the day as possible, not to mention wearing him out so he wouldn't be pecking me on the head about minutiae first thing in the morning.

I sent him to senior centers laden with donuts, to the Rotary Club, the Lions, Knights of Columbus, the Chamber of Commerce, mom-and-pop grocery stores, shopping malls . . . Three nights a week, I'd have him going door to door for two hours with the volunteers. He called bingo every few weeks and sat for interviews on the worst brand of public-access cable (one Armenian guy with a ludicrous mustache and thick accent insisted he could turn his community against us if Martini didn't appear on his show). At one event he shot the starter pistol at a road race and ended up deafening himself for an hour.

Though we weren't paying for publicity with campaign funds during that period, Martini was reaping the benefits of the $15 million charitable foundation of which he was the sole trustee. Ironically, the need for charitable grants was greatest among Klein's supporters. When the foundation donated $42,000 to a hospital in the ethnic lower-income areas that historically swung Democratic, it was reasonable to hope that noncommitted voters in that community would stay home on Election Day, whether or not the gift left them with an actual warm feeling about Martini. When the foundation gave an urban church in that neighborhood $5,000, my hope was it meant one less reverend preaching from the pulpit for Klein.

Within the Republican base, the foundation's charitable grants had the extra benefit of giving us a fighting chance to win over the right-wing fringe for Martini, who didn't necessarily have all the qualifications for getting the full benefit of the troglodyte vote. Martini was pro-choice with restrictions, and not a gun freak; these "lapses" meant that the hard-core right-wingers were not going to be enthused about his candidacy and might not vote at all. But a foundation grant, such as funds to fix a pipe organ, or a grant for a recreation department, could help the word get around that Martini was a friendly. The best outcome, as I saw it, was that some of the nuts even surmised that Martini was disguising his true winger identity due to the district's demographics.

By the time Klein finally launched his attack that October, the race had already gone far beyond ugly. Once each side had begun airing its paid ads and mailing out all the libel they could print, the papers were feigning disgust for both camps while eagerly devouring every slanderous dish we served them. The dirtier things got, the more I liked our odds. When it came to playing in the gutter, we were the professionals—the Dems weren't even junior varsity.

"Klein and Martini have assaulted each other with a special fervor," reported the Bergen County *Record* at the time. "Both men are millionaires who reported raising over $700,000 through mid-October. They are spending heavily in the last month on radio, television, direct mail, and phone banks to define their own image and tear down the opponent's self-definitions."

For our part, we were hacking away at Klein's appeal to blue-collar whites and Latinos by playing up his "support" for illegal aliens in mailers that featured photos of immigrant mobs climbing over and tearing down border fences. We laid it on especially thick in the Puerto Rican community, under the theory that no one north of the Mason-Dixon hates illegal Mexicans and Cubans with quite the same passion as a natural-born Puerto Rican. Klein's ads were still chanting his mantra that Martini had "handed out Get Out of Jail Free cards" to all sorts of monsters when, on October 17, the *North Jersey Herald & News* reported that his camp was about to run a radio spot slamming Martini for taking "a huge haul" of $1,400 from Larry Tromeur.

When the reporters started calling, I merely asked them, "If Tromeur is such an unsavory character, why did Representative Klein accept five hundred dollars from him?" Then I floated a term that I knew would eat away at every fiber of the enemy's campaign like an angry cancer: "hypocrite."

Almost immediately, Klein's camp went dark. What little Klein said to defend himself only made him sound like even more of an ass, trying to explain how the same contribution source can be tainted in one case and not in another—within the very same election. I could only have been happier if we'd caught him touching small children. One day he was poised to deliver us a deathblow, the next he was a hypocritical bureaucrat so detached from reality that he didn't know where his own money came from. Of course, he was only detached from the reality that I had created for him, and that made it even sweeter.

The next round of polls showed a statistical dead heat, but we were still in the fight and I had no intention of losing momentum to the man I'd just knocked down. It being October, we needed some special little gift to put us over the top. And one statement Martini made to the press in the wake of the Tromeur fiasco should have let Klein know that we were just in the process of tying a bow around it: "If he wants to start talking about conduct, he'd better be prepared to defend his own."

One afternoon three weeks before the election, I had Martini out visiting a hospital and I was enjoying his absence. I was grinding away in the office when Martini called from his car. I could hear in his voice that he was struggling to maintain his composure.

"I just had an interesting run-in at that last campaign stop."

"Great," I said, thinking, There goes my afternoon. Martini probably just re-refined his position on Medicare and wanted to spend three hours telling me about it.

"I'll fill you in when I get back to the office," he threatened.

"Well, fuck," I said, hanging up. If he'd done it over the phone, I could at least have worked on something else while he chattered on. But no, he had to do the whole performance. The next thing I knew, he was sidling up to me and rushing me into his office.

As usual, he had to flip through his spiral notebooks before he could start. "I had an interesting conversation at St. Mary's," he began matter-of-factly. "I ran into this guy."

"Okay?"

"So I'm walking through the hospital with the doctor and meeting nurses and patients, we're talking about fucking health care and, you know, like that, when this guy gets my attention—this little crippled guy." Here Martini starts hamming it up for me, hunching his shoulders and wrapping his hands around the handle of an imaginary cane. He also had this way of excitedly bouncing like a little kid with a secret whenever he was about to start telling you something weird or unusual.

"Well, this cripple calls me over, he's there for physical therapy, he tells me—a little guy in a hospital gown with a cane and a beard. He's all bent over and he whispers to me, 'Are you running against Herb Klein?' "

Now I'm actually getting intrigued, but I know better than to interrupt Martini and risk sending him off on a tangent from which he might never return.

"So he says, 'Good. I hate that piece of shit!' " Now, a lot of candidates would have blown the man off as a whack job and moved on, but Bill Martini loved a good story. With Martini's encouragement and undivided attention, "Hospital Gown," as we affectionately came to know him, told the tale that would put Klein's campaign in the ground once and for all.

"It just so happens that this guy was working as a valet at a social club in Hudson County when Herb Klein got into his car around midnight one night and ran him over."

I let it set in for a fraction of a second. "He ran the guy over?"

"Ran him over? He dragged the poor son of a bitch all over the fucking parking lot! The guy's a mess. He's got fucking brain damage, the works!"

Now I was taken aback. It was a whole new paradigm. "This is a miracle!" I said. "It's unbelievable!"

I had been thinking for weeks that we'd have to come up with something to end Klein's political career. Having something as simple as the truth to do it for us was a total boon. Still, the truth needs the most careful handling of all; it always comes with a lot of inconvenient facts that could lessen its value in the hands of an amateur. We were obviously going to drop this thing on Klein's head like a flaming sack, but I had to figure out precisely how to go about it.

"So," I said, "tell me more about Hospital Gown."

"Herb mowed the guy down like a dog! Broken bones, neural injuries, the whole nine."

"And how did we not read about this?"

Again, the Wild Bill grin appeared. "That's the beauty part, Allen. It happened seven years ago."

That was beautiful indeed. Seven years of silence could mean only one thing: cover-up. And a cover-up always comes along with its partner: the payoff. "So why would Hospital Gown tell you all this?" I asked.

"I guess it's like he said. He hates Klein. I'm telling you, this guy came outta the blue, never saw him before in my life. The case was sealed in civil litigation. He reached a settlement and the court sealed the case."

"Klein got it sealed?" I said. "It's perfect! I love it!"

"I thought you would." Getting a traffic case sealed wasn't just uncommon, it was almost unheard of. And the best part? "Klein just got it sealed last year."

I immediately understood the ramifications. Not only did this asshole run a man down outside of some back-alley social club in one of the most mobbed-up sections of New Jersey, he then waited six years, and, while a sitting congressman, got it all wiped from the public record on the eve of his reelection.

Next, Martini offered me the coup de grâce: "Hospital Gown wasn't just a valet. He also used to work for the Hudson County Sheriff's Department."

"He was a cop? Klein hit a cop?"

"He runs down a cop! Can you believe this fucking guy?"

This thing was the Blob—it just kept growing.

"We need to get this in the papers," I said. "Herb Klein ran down a cop—a *hero* cop—at a backroom Mafia joint, shut him up with a few greasy nickels, and then used his office to bury it. It writes itself! Will Hospital Gown talk to the press?"

"No. I told you, it's sealed. He hates Klein, but he's got a financial agreement."

"Then it's too bad for him that he opened his mouth. We've got to get that police report."

I spent the next week trying to track down that document. The Hudson County sheriff had nothing, the county courthouse had nothing. The Motor Vehicles Commission? Nothing. It was like it disappeared off the face of the earth. It simply didn't exist. When Martini called me into his office to ask how the search was going, I told him, "I've got nothing."

"Where'd you look?"

"Everywhere."

He got a gleam in his eye whenever he was about to let something drop. Sliding a file across the desk, he said, "This is what we were looking for."

I didn't even ask how he got his hands on that police report–better that I didn't know–but all the gory details were there. The names, location, time of incident . . . there was even a stick-figure diagram illustrating the poor bastard's trip around the lot while stuck under Klein's car.

"Can you believe this?" Martini said. "Can you fucking *believe* this? I can just see Klein dragging this guy around the parking lot."

"It's all here," I said. "But we need to figure out how to make the most of it. This isn't something you just stick in a piece of mail with a picture of a car on top of a cop."

Martini started wringing his hands. "I wish we could get this guy to hobble over for a press conference." I suggested getting the sheriff, a Republican, to release it for us, but Martini didn't think he'd go for it, explaining, "He runs the county. He doesn't care about Congress and he doesn't care much for me."

So we reviewed. We couldn't hold a press conference, we couldn't come up with anyone to release it for us, and it wasn't something we could test out with a survey as an excuse to get into the public domain, since we already knew the answer to the question, "Would you be more likely or less likely to vote for a candidate who ran over a police officer?" But we had to use it. It was toxic. As far as I was concerned, it would be irresponsible *not* to use it.

The only thing left to do was to leak it ourselves. We discussed which of three local papers to give it to. The *Herald & News* was friendly toward us, the *Newark Star-Ledger* was barely even covering the race, and the Bergen *Record*'s guy was exacerbating; he would ask a lot of penetrating-in-the-wrong-way questions. In the end, I figured it had to be everywhere. This late in the game, there was no reason to alienate any two papers by letting the third scoop them.

"Besides," I pointed out, "why deny half the voters in the district the opportunity to read this article?"

"I can't wait to see the look on this fucking guy's face. Steam's gonna come out of his ears. Am I right?"

I was in full gunslinger mode myself. "No freaking way Klein's told his people about this. Why would he? It would've been better for him if he'd just fucking killed the guy."

The only question left was when to drop it. The Friday before the election, the papers go black. We decided to drop it ten days before the polls opened, to give it time to sink in. We weren't looking for one day of press. What we wanted was nine days of Herb Klein crippling this hero cop. We'd leak it on Thursday, let it carry into Monday, and it would be all Klein had left to talk about through the last week of the election campaign.

Before we could leak it, I had to figure out exactly how to frame the issue for the reporters, who would inevitably ask, "Just what are you accusing him of?"

Well, it made him look like an asshole, for starters. Did anyone want to vote for a guy driving around like Pac-Man in a social club parking lot? Moreover, when we were done shaping it, it would be about character. It wasn't merely that Klein wasn't honest—who's honest? It was that he wasn't candid. An elected official has to maintain the appearance of candor. Not only didn't Klein want to explain his mistakes, he didn't want anyone to know they even existed. Or so I would explain to our friends in the press.

I invited David Voreacos from the Bergen *Record*, Keith Ryzewicz from the *North Jersey Herald & News,* and the beat reporter from the *Newark Star-Ledger* to the storefront headquarters, and left a standing order with the rest of the campaign workers that no one, under any circumstances, should come to the storefront before noon. I put two folding tables together to form a square conference table, put out coffee and donuts, and locked all the doors. As each reporter arrived, I unlocked the door and then locked it again behind them. Meanwhile, Martini was timing his entrance from the back office and wasn't telling anyone why they were there.

The reporters didn't make small talk, and they seemed pretty annoyed. Nine-thirty in the morning is appallingly early for a local political hack. Finally, Voreacos said, "What are we doing here?"

"It's a good story," was all I said. "I think you're going to enjoy reporting it."

"Well, I've got things to do."

Just then, Martini came out, and I announced, "You all understand that this is all off the record and not for attribution."

"I can't agree to that," Voreacos said. "I'll listen to what you have to say, and if I have to cite who it comes from, I'll tell you."

We went back and forth on that for a while. Our hope had been to get this into the papers on deep background so we wouldn't be seen as mudslingers. Deep background is a great tool for feeding information to lazy journalists who want stories to fall into their laps rather than sweating the rigorous investigative work that can turn up a gem. Unfortunately for us, David Voreacos wasn't as lax as we had hoped.

In the end, there wasn't a lot of sense in sticking to our guns on the issue. People would know where the attack came from, whether the papers initially linked it to us or not. And we had gone so far by then that we were counting on voters to be more repelled by Klein's actions than by our revealing them.

Martini opened up with: "I want to discuss Herbert Klein and his conduct both as a politician and as the House Member from New Jersey's Eighth Congressional District."

There was a little rhubarbing back and forth—"This sounds interesting."

"I had contact with a gentleman who had a traffic altercation," he continued, and the hounds caught the scent. They started furiously scribbling in their notebooks. Martini gave me the cue, and I handed out copies of the police report.

"What you have before you is a report from the Hudson County Sheriff's Department," Martini told them.

With that, you could almost feel the temperature of the room change. They were all looking at us differently now. The look on Voreacos's face said, "I can't believe you're going there!" The *Herald & News* guy was salivating.

What I thought then was, This is what I signed on for. This is what I've been working toward all along. With this one act, I had become a whole new caliber of hired gun. I could see it in the reporters' faces.

I went through the whole conversation with them.

"This isn't about an accident," I told them. "This is about the conduct of a sitting congressman after the fact." As we had planned, I started using Klein's own words against him. "He says he's for transparency in government, but just last year he had this file taken out of the public domain. What kind of transparency is that? The injury is not the issue. This is all about how he conducted himself as a congressman in anticipation of reelection."

"How did you find this?" Voreacos asked. At that point, he was the only one in the room who cared about such mundane details.

"It came to us origin unknown."

"Can you get in touch with the victim?"

"Yes, but I can't tell you how to."

"Has he contacted you?"

Here I had to be careful. We couldn't attack Klein's lack of candor if we were going to be seen as hiding and taking potshots. We were claiming all along that we had nothing to hide. So Martini finally confessed, "The victim called me back in June."

What an artist the man was! His mistruths came in layers—they came in thirty-one flavors! I started piecing it together while Martini fed it to the reporters. The hospital story he'd told me was true, but it had happened five months ago. He'd been planning this whole thing and waited until the polls had us in a dead heat to use it. Thinking back to the act he'd treated me to in his office, I didn't know whether to be horrified or impressed.

In the end, I couldn't help but admire the man.

"At first, I took it for rumor," Martini was saying, "but then this report was delivered to us . . . as Allen said, origin unknown. It doesn't exist on the record. We've also discovered through the MVC that Representative Klein's driving record is so bad he had to get a special state-sponsored insurance policy. No private company will cover him. Is this what the people bargained for? He's using his power to seal cases and hide the past. What else might he do?"

Finally, Martini went on the record: "To cause the disposition of a civil court proceeding to be taken out of the public domain while he is a sitting congressman does not fall within Mr. Klein's own stated principles."

"At this point," I followed up, "questions have to be answered by Mr. Klein. You have to ask him for answers. We certainly don't have any."

Voreacos had just one follow-up question. "Why are you releasing this?"

"For the last four weeks he's been discrediting Bill's professional career," I said, "and everyone knows Bill's record is unblemished. But the people of the district should know who these attacks come from. You're attacking Bill Martini? Who are you when you look in the mirror? This incident is very instructive. The voters have a right to know what Klein is up to."

With that, we wanted to get out of the way and never speak of it again. We wanted Herb Klein to call us liars, to sound hyper and re-actionary. He gave us everything we asked for.

At six-thirty the next morning, the ringing phone woke me up. It was Martini wanting to know if I had seen the papers.

"The papers? It's six-thirty, Bill."

"So what are you doing? Get to work!"

I waded through the media frenzy back at the office. Voreacos was his usual unbiased self, under a totally sexless headline, "Martini Criticizes Klein Over Civil Suit." But the *Record* came through all the way with the purely satisfying "Klein-Martini Race Turns Uglier!" Uglier, who figured? Certainly not Klein. The article began, "Life in the fast lane. . . ."

Klein went batshit. "Martini must be hallucinating!" he howled to the papers. "This is desperate, despicable, and dumb. This has no relevance. It's so childlike it doesn't even merit a response."

We must have spent hours reading those stories over and over again, savoring every word. Klein was trying to make us out to be a bunch of lying thugs, but the reporters had done their jobs. They had spent the day researching, and had spoken to all the attorneys involved.

Hospital Gown freaked out almost as badly as Klein himself. "I don't know anything," he told the reporters. "It's sealed. I can't talk to you."

We were reading the papers' description of him and laughing our asses off. "A frail, bearded man who walks with a cane. He's had neurological damage." We high-fived each other. "It could only be better if he'd gotten both his legs chopped off!"

Yes, I was a dick. That was my job, and I was pretty good at it—and learning every day.

I secretly had "Hit and Run Herb" splashed across the fronts of T-shirts in screaming letters and handed them out to the volunteers to wear at the upcoming final debate. On the back was printed, "You can't trust him behind the wheel of a car. Can you trust him in Congress?"

Martini would never talk about those shirts, but I explained to the press that we couldn't stop a grassroots uprising from making them. Hey, it's basic freedom of expression, First Amendment, right?

And what did we get for all that plotting? What was our prize for all that media manipulation? What tsunami effect did we generate by ruining one man's credibility while possibly wrecking the financial future of a handicapped ex-cop?

Martini won the election by just over 5,000 votes.

With margins that thin, there's no room for gentlemen. It reaches a point where not taking every available swing at your opponent is actually the irresponsible thing. Your candidate is paying you to bring in votes, not to be their priest or psychologist. Every vote has a specific monetary value, and every one that you let slip away is money you've stolen. The minute you lose sight of that, you've lost the whole game.

Martini was just one of thirty-four Republicans who replaced their Democratic rivals in Congress in our Republican Revolution, and I can guarantee you that the tactics Martini and I used were not any kind of exception that year or in all the years thereafter.

In fact, as dirty as the game I played for Martini was, it would look like a sorority tickle fight compared to the campaigns that followed.

SIX

*I*t was a hell of a time to be a newly arriving Republican in Washington when Martini and I showed up. Our Party had just wrested control of the House and Senate from a bunch of tax-and-spend liberals and we were going to set things straight once and for all. Now that the Republicans had arrived we were going to stand as one for the good of all America—if by "one" you meant "Southern Republicans," and if by "America" you meant "Southern Republicans."

I had barely set up shop before I discovered that Newt Gingrich and his fellow "Southern Strategy" revolutionists considered moderate Republicans from the North like Martini and me to be, at best, remnants of a gloomy bygone era, or—more often than not—part of the problem. Through all the coming struggles, I would have to keep one thing in mind above all else: my own career.

Getting Martini elected fulfilled the first part of the ludicrous five-year plan I'd dreamed up in grad school. Step two was simple enough: I would just become Martini's chief of staff.

"Look," I told him. "I want to go to Washington. I want to be your chief of staff."

"Well," he said, "we'll see. We'll see."

We'll *see*? What the hell was that? My elation at Martini's victory dried up in the face of his being such an ungrateful megalomaniac—that is to say, a total politician. I'd just put in six months for the guy seven days a week. There had been no long weekends, no weekends at all, just half a year of hitting the office by seven-thirty in the morning and rarely going home before midnight. Now here's Bill Martini, the freshman congressman from New Jersey, ascending to the seat of power, and me with no fucking life. Elizabeth and I were engaged and I'd barely seen her since I proposed. I was living in a crappy little apartment in Montclair, New Jersey, which I'd chosen because I knew I would always want to be in the office during the campaign, and now it seemed I could just stay there as far as Martini was concerned.

He actually made me go through the paces of interviewing people for the chief of staff job, my job—a job he wouldn't have been able to offer anyone if not for me.

Okay, I thought, I'll find some job applicants for you. I spent the next three weeks personally rounding up the worst specimens I could find. Basically, I was looking for a guy in clown shoes, suspenders, and a funny hat. This being Washington, I found plenty of them. Only after I had paraded about half a dozen dribbling imbeciles past Martini's desk did he finally relent.

"Okay, okay," he said. "I get the message. You got the job."

"Great. What are you going to pay me?"

"I'm gonna start you at sixty thousand." He announced the sum as if it was something a man would dash into a burning building to claim. Most congressional chiefs of staff at the time were starting at $90,000 and the top players were making around $140,000.

"Sixty thousand?" I said. "Where did you come up with a number like that?"

"Hey, I thought you'd be happy. That's *twice* what you're making right now!"

"But it's not even on the same scale as what everyone else is making."

He started fidgeting with his ever-present stack of papers, say-ing, "Well, that's the job. Take it or leave it." So he was giving me what I wanted, but sticking it to me at the same time. Still, as had been the case throughout my career to that point, my salary was not a huge issue for me; rather it was the constant need to rise up through the system. Despite Bill bending me over on the money, I was psyched. Elizabeth was already down in D.C. finishing up grad school and I was going to join her so we could finally start our life to-gether. As far as I knew, I was getting everything I wanted.

The Martini team we put together in Washington was a motley crew. The first guy we hired was Leslie Novitsky, who had been the exec-utive assistant to Representative Michael Huffington, the one-term Republican congressman from California who had just lost a Senate bid despite having set the record in that campaign for the most per-sonal wealth ever spent on a nonpresidential race. When I told Les-lie that he had the job, he said, "This is great—I finally get to work with normal people!"

I didn't know much about the Huffingtons, but I did know that this guy stood very little chance of surviving Martini Land if he was looking for "normal people."

Life under Bill Martini was incredibly demanding. The level of work product that Bill expected from his people at all times was akin to that of a district attorney preparing a capital murder case. Except Bill's trials never ended. The rest of us were battle-hardened from the campaign, and we all respected Bill because he worked harder than any of us, but the new guy just couldn't hack the pace of things.

After just a couple of weeks there came a Monday when Leslie wasn't to be found. I tried to raise him on the phone but his machine kept picking up. Tuesday rolled by and I still hadn't seen or heard from the guy. It was late November, we were preparing for the swearing-in ceremony in January, which included organizing a group of two hundred supporters to come down to D.C. from New

Jersey—and our office manager had disappeared from the face of the earth.

That Wednesday afternoon, I happened to drop my pen and it rolled under our fax machine. Crouching down and reaching under the fax, I pulled out a crumpled piece of paper. It was a fax from Leslie that read, "I just can't do this again. I resign."

I later found out that he'd been so terrified of Bill that he had retreated all the way to his mother's house in Florida to hide out.

To Bill, my most important task before the swearing-in ceremony was to score him a choice office on Capitol Hill. His marching orders were that his personal office had to have an exit he could slip out of without having to pass through the reception area, in case anyone he didn't want to see was waiting for him there. He required an escape hatch.

Unfortunately for me, freshman members are given offices by lottery and we were way down near the bottom of the list. I was given two choices: a dismal, cagelike converted attic on the fifth floor of the Cannon House Office Building that featured Bill's obligatory escape hatch; or a beautiful, spacious corner office on the fifth floor of the Longworth House Office Building that was composed of two parallel suites of rooms—with a solid brick wall in between them. So if some nagging constituent was lurking outside Bill's member office in the reception area, Bill's only means of getting out unseen would be to smash through a solid brick wall or jump out the window.

Selecting either office would have resulted in the ripping off of my head by Bill Martini. He would just as soon operate out of a phone booth as he would in the dingy attic space we were offered, escape hatch or not.

So I selected the Longworth suites without telling Bill and immediately made an appointment with the House architect.

Indicating the brick wall, I informed the architect, "I'm going to need you to blow a hole in this."

He did just that.

My first official act as a congressional chief of staff was to take a piece of American history and blow it up, all in the name of allowing a congressman to evade the face-to-face scrutiny of the fellow citizens who elected him. It seemed to me that whatever we'd be doing in the federal government, it would probably be something we'd want at all costs to avoid being questioned about.

I watched the swearing-in, the handing of the gavel from Dick Gephardt to Newt Gingrich, on a TV in the Speaker's office, which was still cluttered with debris left behind by the previous occupant. It felt entirely appropriate. I didn't have my hands on the levers of national power, but I was finally in a place where I could see them being worked with my own eyes. I had a security pass that let me roam anywhere I wanted in the Capitol. I was twenty-eight and one of the youngest in my position on the Hill. It was wild.

My lofty musings about history being made, and my own place in that history, lasted about as long as the swearing-in ceremony. After that, it was back to earth, where Congressman Bill Martini had to start raising money pronto. That is the main job of a member of Congress and it takes up more of their time and effort than anything else. They can do some other things as well, so long as those things don't get in the way of the fund-raising.

That's not necessarily an indictment of the system. You can't get reelected without money, and if you can't get reelected you can't do *anything*. And there's no person or party in the world you can blame this on. If you tried to, they'd just hand you the old joke: "What are you looking at me for? *I* didn't write the Constitution!"

So every politician needs piles of money, but Bill needed a mountain of it. He was from a Democratic district and a presidential election year was on the horizon, which meant that turnout was going to be high. High turnout was the last thing Bill needed. We were going to have to work very hard not to lose.

One thing Bill had in his favor was that he landed on the Transportation Committee. If you're on the Transportation Committee, the oil and trucker lobbyists will come bearing checks.

When the Exxon lobbyists came looking for Bill, he didn't want to take a meeting, but he did want to take their money, so I subbed for him.

I brought them into my little section of the office, where they proceeded to try to get me to tell them the congressman's position on an upcoming bill. All I could do was dance around the issue, since Bill still hadn't taken a position.

I kept saying, "Well, I think the congressman this," and "I think the congressman that," until one of them finally got fed up.

"Look, we don't really care what you think; we care what he thinks. We want to talk to him, so why don't we just reschedule this meeting?"

"Okay, that's fine."

"Oh, and we brought something for you." With that, the Exxon lobbyist took a blank envelope from his briefcase and held it toward me, but I wouldn't take it. I'd just gone through this whole ethics course as part of my orientation program, where they told us that it's illegal to accept a check on government property.

What with all of our GOP talk about getting the Contract with America signed in the first hundred days and reforming business as usual in Congress and all that bullshit, I was feeling patriotic.

"Is that a check?" I asked.

"Well, yeah. It's a check."

I was aghast. "You know I can't take that check."

The lobbyist was dumbstruck. "Um, okay. Well, would you like to arrange for some other—"

"Tell you what. I'll walk you down."

That was my solution. I rode down in the elevator with them, walked them outside, and literally stepped off the curb and into the street.

"All right," I said, "I can take the check now."

He looked at me like I was out of my mind, then handed over

the check. I thought I couldn't have been more aboveboard: I was complying with the letter of the law and that was enough. Of course, I found out later that it isn't enough by a long shot.

Another reason why my sensation of being in a position of power faded so quickly is that Bill Martini and I didn't have any power at all. Sure, there was the Republican Revolution, but we were the wrong kind of Republicans.

The right kind of Republican could only be found in the South and Midwest, and Newt Gingrich was their exalted leader. I learned in my first meeting with Newt that he was a very bright guy, and that he went off on impossible tangents. Sometimes he asked an awful lot by expecting you to stick with him. During a member orientation meeting, he started talking about the future, the Contract with America, and the next hundred days—and before I knew it he was discussing the possibility of farming on Mars.

His plan for farming on Mars wasn't the only strange thing about the meeting, since Newt had decorated the center of his office with a humongous *Tyrannosaurus rex* skull that he'd borrowed from the Smithsonian. You could hardly stand anywhere in the room without brushing up against its Plexiglas case. I made myself crazy trying to imagine what the symbolism behind it was. Were the Democrats now the dinosaurs, doomed to go out of existence entirely? Or were we the dinosaurs and they the puny little mammals we were going to devour? Either way, it wasn't the most heartening piece of furniture I'd ever seen.

No one had bothered to tell me that Newt dabbled in amateur paleontology.

Newt and his gang of core Republicans were worse than heavy-handed. As far as they were concerned, the Southern Strategy was the sole explanation for the Republican takeover of the legislature. To myself and my fellow Northeastern Republicans, the impression was: "We're fucked."

The guys from the South had no concept of our needs. To them we were the last of the dodo birds. "Who needs them? We're the future. We're the Southern Strategy!"

The moderate Republican cause of smaller government and responsible pay-as-you-go fiscal policy wasn't helped much when Sonny Bono got up to speak at a conference for freshman members. "When you're sitting in the big chair," he told us, "you've got everyone's fate in your hands."

"How in God's name," we wondered, "did this nutty hippie get to be one of us?"

He talked about being mayor of Palm Springs, California, which is like being the mayor of Shangri-la—it's all old rich people and no schools to pay for. But at least Sonny had some kind of vision of good government—that taking control of the legislature was an opportunity to improve the whole country, not an invitation to jam ultraconservative dogma down its throat. Of course, most of the GOP freshman class of 1994 weren't ready to hear it because they were still celebrating and feeling invincible. That the rest of America wasn't as enthusiastic as the newly minted Republican congressional majority was just not what the Southern Strategy adherents wanted to hear.

Anyone who thought that good government was about compromise, about working with the other side, negotiating their principles to get something done—they were out of business. The Southerners just weren't going to do that. They had a mandate. Their strategy was to play to the base at all costs.

There was always a palpable sense that we were being held in contempt by our colleagues from the Southern and mountain states. Somehow you were less of a Republican if you tended toward compromise.

How, for instance, could Bill Martini be unabashedly pro–railroad union? Gee, lemme think . . . maybe it's because there's a crapload of railroad union members in our district? This type of logic was somehow lost on our Southern Strategy comrades.

Above all, the Newt boys expected you to shut up and fall in line. I was always resentful that they considered the Republican majority to be their doing. They had almost nothing to do with our New Jersey win. In fact, their pro-life, snake-handling babble could have easily cost us the election, but if you tried to tell that to Newt and his followers they'd march on your office bearing pitchforks and torches. Their special brand of religious doggerel might go over in Oklahoma, but try selling the stuff to a bunch of Springsteen fans in Asbury Park.

It would have been one thing if the meatheads were only telling Martini to snap to when it came to votes on federal funding for abortion—which he wouldn't—but they didn't stop there. Martini offered a pay-go bill that would have required the House to pass a spending cut to offset each tax cut that got passed. That meant trouble. Moderate Republicans are about balancing budgets and reducing government spending; neocon Republicans are about cutting taxes no matter what the result. If only their crusading ended there.

The leadership went nuts. They said, in a nutshell, "No! There's not a one-to-one ratio. Tax cuts are more important!" They didn't want to bother with the exercise of finding responsible ways to cut taxes. This is where Bill started to find his ground. He teamed up with fellow Republican congressmen Mike Castle of Delaware and Fred Upton of Michigan to challenge the neocons on the issue. In the end the pay-go budget rule, requiring that revenue and spending legislation be deficit neutral, passed because its common sense overwhelmed the stubbornness of Southern Strategy tax-cut dogma.

But in the end it came down to a simple choice: vote with the leadership or have your ass handed to you. Any representative who didn't vote the Party line was useless to the Party, and therefore couldn't count on getting any fund-raising help from it. These days Republican candidates have the luxury of wanting the top man in the Party to stay the hell away from their campaigns, but back then it was a big deal. If you played nice on votes and Newt consented to visit your district you could raise $50,000 in a day—again, if you played nice. For unrepentant offenders there were worse punishments . . . like waking up one day and finding that your committee assignment had been taken away.

So every time Bill Martini wanted to vote his conscience, he had to ask himself, "Can I take the hit?"

Any member of Congress can talk about responsible spending when he's standing up against pork barrel spending in someone else's district, but Martini was one of the few who fought it in his own. Robert Roe, the Democrat who had represented the 8th District for twenty years before Herb Klein's one term, had finagled Congress into funding a $1.8 billion construction project to build a flood tunnel in his home county. Now Roe was a consultant on the project, raking in his cut. Neither party has ever cornered the market on this kind of shit.

Bill had rallied against the tunnel throughout his campaign. "Why should we be spending two billion dollars to save a few houses on a flood plain?" he asked voters. What we all wanted to say was "Who told them to build houses on a flood plain in the first place?" But we kept it to the more solemn "This is important to the families affected, but there are better, less expensive options to consider." Meaning, we'll let you know what those changes are after we get to Congress. And then you can go screw.

Bill might have lost 260 votes in the neighborhood with the flood tunnel, but he picked up thousands across the district. Now that he was in Congress, one of his first orders of business was to take away Roe's meal ticket. Roe didn't go away easily. He called Bill to a number of meetings to "educate" him on the importance of the Passaic River Flood Tunnel. But considering that by that time we'd already dropped a hundred thousand pieces of mail and spent tens of thousands of dollars on cable television and radio condemning the project as wasteful spending—combined with the fact that the rest of the GOP majority in the 104th Congress was willing to oblige Martini in sacrificing his own pork at the altar of fiscal responsibility—the public teat dried up on Mr. Roe's flood tunnel and it died a pitiful death.

· · ·

Despite that victory, Martini was always being told what to do by the Southern Insurgency. And Martini was used to telling other people what to do. This new experience of having a pack of backwoods hayseeds giving him marching orders daily did not jibe well with his sense of self. He got into the habit of saying "I have to go see the Speaker and get my ass chewed out." These chewing-outs were always member-to-member, private affairs. But whenever you heard that someone was having a meeting with Newt, it meant that he or she was getting dressed down.

Every time Bill would come back from such a meeting, he'd tell me, "I've only got half an ass left."

I knew not to ask the specifics, but I could see the results.

Bill's screaming fits were reaching exciting new heights all the time. I remember going into his office one day to tell him that two nuns from the district had shown up without an appointment and were currently waiting for him on the other side of the door. I had barely told him about the penguins when he started shouting, "I'm a ball of fire!" while repeatedly slamming a wooden inbox against his desk.

The inbox smashed to pieces, Bill was clutching splinters in both fists and huffing, "This press release isn't good enough. What are you gonna do about it? What are you gonna do about it?"

"I guess I'm going to get you a new inbox."

"Goddammit!"

With that he proceeded to storm out of the office using the escape hatch. Bill knew he didn't want the nuns seeing him in such a state. But the nuns heard it all through the paper-thin walls.

"I'm sorry," I told the sisters, whose eyes were as big as saucers by then. "The congressman is a little disappointed about a vote that didn't go his way. Would you like to schedule an appointment?"

Martini's need for an escape hatch suddenly made perfect sense to me. I started looking for one of my own.

My work schedule was the same 24/7 grind it had been on the

campaign, but there was no longer a winnable campaign. There was no workable end in sight. Bill was going to lose in '96. There was just no way that he was going to survive a presidential year. In the end, it just wouldn't matter how much money he raised—there wasn't enough money in the world. In a presidential year, everyone he didn't want to see turning up at the polls would turn up—namely, minorities. As far as my career was concerned, I already had the credit for his win; if I didn't stick around for the impending massacre, I'd also get credit for being smart enough to pull out ahead of time.

I knew I would be leaving the Martini camp as soon as the first good opportunity presented itself, so my final stretch as chief of staff was yet another waiting game in my career. If Bill wasn't haranguing me, it was some constituent. If it wasn't a constituent complaining about something, it was some staff member. In the meantime, Elizabeth and I had gotten married over the summer and I had rarely set eyes on her since I was driving, training, and flying back and forth between New Jersey and D.C. every few days.

What I despised most of all, though, was the Capitol Hill culture itself. I'd been through prep school, college, grad school, and nearly half a dozen campaigns, yet I'd never seen such a cliquish bunch of self-obsessed boors as I found roaming the bars and restaurants and social clubs of Washington, D.C. If you were a chief of staff, it was expected that you would socialize only among fellow chiefs of staff. It was the same for legislative directors, press secretaries, staff assistants, and so on down the line. You really weren't supposed to mingle with anyone who had a job title different than yours.

To me, it was just idiotic. The artificial social confinements so annoyed me that after almost a year in Washington, I still hadn't developed a network of colleagues. Besides, I was so exhausted at the end of the day that I just wanted to go home and pass out rather than schmooze. On the rare occasions that I had some free time, I wanted to hang out with Elizabeth, watch TV, see a movie—anything that smacked of having a life.

My main problem in D.C. was that I never quite bought the total package; I never finished my Kool-Aid. I had already spent four years in college completely loaded—at the conclusion of which I showed up shitfaced to an art history exam after wrapping my car around a telephone pole—so the after-work bar crawls never appealed to me. But you can't get by in Washington on the half-package tour. People sense that you don't want to play the game and they naturally don't gravitate toward you. I knew I was missing out on a lot of opportunities by keeping socially aloof, but that had always been my weakness politically. Besides, something always seemed to turn up at the right time.

It was October 1995 when I got another call from Bill Ulrey, my old boss at the New Jersey Republican State Committee who had hooked me up with the Ellen Harley campaign in Pennsylvania—though I didn't hold that against him. Ulrey was now chief of staff for New Jersey congressman Bob Franks, who'd gotten into the House through a special election in '92. Ulrey told me he had just been offered a job with the Republican National Committee, and that he didn't want it.

"But I recommended you," he said. "I think you might be getting a phone call."

That call from the RNC was a godsend. Though I had wanted to quit my job for months, I didn't have a lot of spectacular options. I couldn't just quit and hope to find a viable candidate in the upcoming elections whose campaign I could manage; the few that existed were already spoken for. The culture was, and is, such that a guy like me who wanted to manage campaigns couldn't just hop from one incumbent race to another. Incumbents had their own people and were not inclined to add new faces; that inevitably meant new opinions and methods, which was the last thing they wanted if they'd already succeeded. Ninety-five percent of incumbents win because they make the laws of how elections are waged. Moreover, their staffs know this and tend to protect their positions; bringing in a new team member makes the pool of advancement opportunities smaller, so it makes no sense to hire a person who could later turn out to be competition for a promotion.

More importantly, if a move was going to happen, I wanted it to be up and not lateral.

The job opening at the RNC was for a regional political director to pursue the Party's interests in the mid-Atlantic region. There were two initial criteria for the position, neither of which I met. First, you had to have run a statewide campaign, or have been the executive director of a state party. I hadn't run a statewide campaign (the Martini race was only districtwide) and I'd never run a state party. You also had to be at least thirty years old, and I was now just twenty-nine. In my favor, I had run a lot of campaigns and I came supplied with a host of recommendations.

My first interview was with the RNC's new political director, Curt Anderson, at his office at the committee headquarters on D Street and First. Anderson had been the RNC's Midwest director during the '94 elections, and had overseen GOP victories in a number of gubernatorial, senatorial, and congressional campaigns. He wanted to gauge my politics. I was a moderate Northeastern Republican walking into the very den of the assault rifle knuckle-draggers. To a movement Republican like Anderson, I was the medicine they were forced to take and not the mint julep they wanted to be sipping. But, as much as it may have pained the RNC, any political director for the mid-Atlantic would have to be someone of my ilk.

My interview with Curt Anderson was unlike any I'd ever had. All through the interview, while I was trying to stay focused, he kept chewing his cigar and making popping noises with his lips. Almost everything he said was either preceded or followed by explosive snort noises coming out of his mouth. And those lip pops were pretty much the only reactions I ever got out of him during the interview. He just asked one loaded question after another, never offering what he thought of my answers. "You ever heard of partial-birth abortion?" *Pop!*

Another thing that distracted me was Anderson's bracelet. It read "WWJD?" In all my time with the GOP I'd never seen such a thing, so I marveled at the specter of a grown man at the height of power wearing a dainty little charm bracelet. When Elizabeth explained the acronym to me that night, I said, "Great, I don't go to church and I married a nice girl who is half Jewish. This should be interesting."

Later I would come to learn that none of the top men or women in the RNC ever asked themselves what Jesus would do until after they got caught doing things he would never have done.

In the end, I guess Anderson found me not *too* offensive for an East Coast Establishment baby-killer, so he scheduled me for an interview the next week with RNC Chairman Haley Barbour. Barbour was the quintessential political old-boy network player from Mississippi. Having taken over the RNC in 1992, his leadership was largely credited with the Republican takeover of '94. He would go on to found what *Fortune* called in 2001 "the most powerful lobbying company in America," before getting himself elected governor of his home state.

Haley was larger than life. It wasn't just that he was a big guy. Sitting in a room with him, you knew you were in the presence of something huge—certainly something larger than yourself. He was also very friendly. Unlike a lot of the Dixie slouches he had helped get elected, Haley was extremely disarming. His interviewing style was easygoing and cordial, as he skillfully utilized his unique blend of Southern charm and zero-sum wisdom. After it had been going on for a while, he asked me, "So have you told Bill Martini that you're talking to us?"

"No, I haven't told him."

"Well, how's he gonna take it if you take this job?"

"You know what?" I remember wondering if what I was about to say was out of line. "He's a big boy," I said. "He'll get over it."

That gave Haley a chuckle. "All right," he said. "You've got the job."

Aside from my disillusionment on discovering that a congressional chief of staff for a freshman congressman has pretty much zero decision-making power and spends the majority of his time getting yammered at by anyone who feels like it, and aside from my disappointment with Washington in general, I was personally pissed at Bill Martini by then. When Elizabeth and I had gotten married that summer, we chartered a forty-two-foot sailboat for just the two of us to sail around the British Virgin Islands. It was our honeymoon, and I hadn't vacationed in years, so I decided to add an extra two days to it. When Martini got wind of the extra time off, he went into a fit, and screamed in front of his entire staff, "What the fuck? He's been fucking her for seven years! What's he need another two days for?"

Despite our squabbles, I know Bill appreciated me and my work ethic. And he was not happy when I broke the news that I was leaving. He started railing against Haley Barbour. "What the hell does he think he's doing, cherry-picking my staff? He works for me!" It proved to him once and for all that the Southern guys just didn't give a rat's ass about the Northeast. And rightly so. The Southern Strategy preempted everything; everything else was the past. If it meant taking away one of their own Party member's personnel, so be it.

Bill's attitude toward me at that point was more or less "All right. Two weeks and you're out of here." I couldn't blame him; I was now part of his past.

The RNC job couldn't have come at a better time. It also came with a $20,000-a-year raise over what Martini was paying me. Still, I knew not to expect much glory.

My region would consist of New York, New Jersey, Maryland, West Virginia, Pennsylvania, Delaware, and D.C., and half those places had nothing going on as far as the Republicans were concerned. No one from the GOP ever showed their face in D.C. outside of their congressional offices; Maryland, Delaware, and West Virginia were generally considered permanently lost to the Democrats. Only New York, New Jersey, and Pennsylvania had real potential for GOP candidates.

The RNC assigned me my seven states and gave me a laptop, a cell phone, and a credit card. Then they said, "Okay, now go do your job." There was no orientation, no job manual. It didn't matter. Haley had given me his calling card in seven states, much like a king giving a lord his new manor.

Rather than being chained to any one campaign or, worse, one candidate, I could ply my trade in elections all across a huge swath of the country. More importantly, Haley's backing meant I was now a full-fledged GOP insider with the clout and opportunity to build a national network of political allies and contacts. Even Newt himself was small beans compared to Haley, because Haley controlled the RNC's money—without which it's all but impossible for a Republican candidate to win an election of any importance. Any Republican running a serious campaign anywhere needed Haley. So, in seven states, that meant they needed me. The next contest would be for all the marbles: continued control of Congress and taking over the White House. Being on Haley's team meant playing a key role, being in the center of the action, and hopefully sharing in the spoils when we won.

I had my portfolio and set off to build my network and future, and maybe do a little work for the Republican National Committee while I was at it.

SEVEN

*T*he regional political director job meant I could fly into any Northeastern state, meet the whole Party apparatus, and say, "Hi, I'm Allen Raymond from the RNC. I'm here to help." My job was to be Haley Barbour's eyes and ears in my assigned region of the country. Haley's regional political directors at the RNC were also supposed to identify crucial congressional, senatorial, and gubernatorial elections and work with the candidates to secure as many Republican victories in a given election cycle as possible. What it really came down to was brokering RNC money from Barbour to the candidates, with us regional directors as the middlemen. That was no small thing, though. Nothing influences politics as severely as money—not even the elections.

Of course, being a professional, the first thing I did was to make sure I got some goodies for my own people in Jersey. I got Peter Murphy, the chairman of the Passaic County Republican Party, a check for $5,000, figuring that Peter was the county chairman in Martini's congressional district and had been helpful to me in 1994, so it couldn't hurt to kiss the ring a little. (Peter was later convicted of mail fraud and bribery and served eleven months in prison before the conviction was overturned on appeal.)

Within a week of starting the job, I got called back to Washington to have dinner with Haley and my new colleagues. These were lavish affairs held every couple of months at renowned restaurants—cocktails by the bucket, surf and turf, the whole thing. All the RNC top brass attended; including Curt Anderson, the RNC political director from that first scary interview; his assistant, Ruth Kistler (who was my main point of contact); and the nine regional political directors. That particular dinner was at Prima Piatti on Pennsylvania Avenue near the White House. Prima Piatti was a newly minted hot spot then, the place to see and be seen, and I liked the idea of being seen there at Haley Barbour's table. One look at his crew and it was clear that at twenty-nine I was by far the baby of the group; the guys from the mountain states and the Southwest were in their fifties, and most of the guys had been at their jobs for two or three years by then. It was a little intimidating. My training with Martini had taught me that, if you don't know the answer to a question, keep your mouth shut unless you're forced to answer.

I was forced.

After a couple of libations, Haley started calling on each of us to give him a status report: "Tommy, what's going on down south?" "Hey, Dave Hanson, give me a rundown from the mountain states." Hanson was a jack Mormon, more jack than Mormon, but he knew his business and left the jack for later in the evening.

Each guy was rattling off campaign data, poll results, and donation figures like it was nothing. By the time Haley called on me, my palms were dripping. I had no idea what to say. My only hope was to play to my strength. They had just had elections in New Jersey, where I actually knew what the hell I was talking about, so I opened with that to kill five or ten minutes. The rest of it was just the bullshit session of the century. I remembered reading something about the Philadelphia mayor's race in the papers, so I tossed that out there. Then I started piecing together the tidbits I had picked up on my first days on the job into a fabric that resembled something like an intelligent briefing about political current events from the Upper East Side of New York to Allegheny County, Pennsylvania. It wasn't fiction, but more like an oral report held together by baling wire and tape—luckily, my experience taught me that the right tone of confidence mixed with enough fact can make one an authority on any subject.

I realized after I'd spoken that it didn't matter what I said. None of those guys cared about the Northeast. As far as they were concerned, West Virginia was Zimbabwe and even D.C. could die in a fire. I also soon realized there was little reason to believe that any of the other field reps had better information about their regions than the nonsense I'd spewed.

Dinner lasted two and a half hours. By the end of it, I was exhausted. As I was leaving, Ruth Kistler came up to me, grabbed my arm, and said, "You did really well."

Great, I thought, at least they don't feel like they just hired a complete idiot.

My fellow regional political directors were all in high spirits, and I had formed the distinct impression they were hard-drinking hacks getting paid a lot to not do a lot.

Shortly after this first (of many) Haley dinners, I got a call from Jim Tobin, the RNC's regional political director for New England, who was based in Maine, where he lived with his wife, Ellen, and their two sons. I'd only met him the night before, but right away he started grilling me. "What's your plan?"

I didn't like that: this person I barely knew coming out of the blue trying to keep tabs on me. The way I saw it, I answered to Haley, or even Curt, but not to the other field reps. Jim Tobin had been at the RNC longer than me, but only by six months. Besides, what good were my plans to him?

I told him, "I guess I'll be going into my states and meeting everyone, try to determine what the most important races are and focus on those." Next, I gave him a pretty detailed account of what

I'd be doing in New Jersey, since I knew the place and had a definite idea of how I was going to dig myself deeper into the state's GOP establishment. My sense was that he was taking notes.

Later, after Tobin and I became friendly, he came down to Washington on RNC business, so Elizabeth and I invited him over for dinner. He showed up bearing Maine lobsters, which we boiled up and feasted on over some wine. During the meal Tobin said, "That first time we talked, after you got hired, you sounded pretty confident." After a pause, he added, "I hated you on that phone call. You'd been there for less than a month and you already sounded like you knew what you were doing." In his six months, he said, he still hadn't figured out what to do.

Jim's career would go on to great heights without his ever quite knowing what to do. And I'd go on to figure that out only after it had cost me my own career.

Even if Haley Barbour's regional political directors seemed to be bumbling in the dark to some extent, Haley never suffered that condition himself. Haley was a master—he knew everything. The guy was an information trap who could tell you the voting returns for municipal dog catcher pretty much anywhere in the country. He would never get caught trying to slide or make shit up.

One of the most important missions I assigned myself was to get a network going in New York State. I didn't know anyone there politically and it was the Big Knish—a huge state with a lot of money and a very competitive Republican Party. The governor, the senior U.S. senator, and the mayor of New York City were all GOP, so it was a critical state for someone like me to do business in. It was also an expensive state to do business in.

What I'd heard is that they didn't give a crap about the RNC in New York. Aside from being almost completely at odds with Southern Strategy Republican ideology, the New York Republicans had their own money. So they made their own rules. If I was going to make headway in Albany, I would need money in my pocket to grease the skids a little. The New York Republicans operated more by money than any other state Party people I met in my region. It is a big state with the largest media market in the world, and given that they had elected a governor and a senator despite New York being generally considered a Democratic state, they were unlikely to turn to me for strategic advice when they had their own seasoned consultants. So the only need left to fill was the coffers. I persuaded Curt Anderson to cut me a check for $5,000. It wasn't a lot, but it was enough to pay the cover charge and two-drink minimum.

To me, Albany was an alien world. Its downtown is a huge governmental metropolis that, in grim weather, quickly assumes the look of some dystopian hellscape. It was foggy the morning I landed and Empire State Plaza's massive gray towers disappearing into the sky reminded me of the half-buried Statue of Liberty in *Planet of the Apes*.

I headed to the New York State Republican Party headquarters and met the chairman, Bill Powers, and Brendan Quinn, the executive director. I could tell from Quinn's body language that he had taken an immediate disliking toward me, so I gave him as much of my shoulder as I could and focused on Powers.

Powers thought I was okay because fifteen minutes into the meeting I said, "I brought you something," and put the check on his desk. After that, he let me hang out in his office all day while he took meetings. It was a good start. Powers was very close with Governor George Pataki and Senator Alfonse D'Amato, and there I was, fresh from D.C., getting introduced to everyone who walked into his office.

Each time a person came in, Powers would say, "This is Al Raymond, the new guy from the RNC. He's a good guy—he just gave me five grand!"

There was no other way. Either you brought money and they tolerated you, or you brought none and they considered you useless. Haley hated that. As far as Haley was concerned, all the money in the RNC should stay in the RNC. If the RNC got a $100,000 donation, it immediately had to kick back $25,000 to whatever state the donor came from. And New York was constantly laying claim to any donor who'd ever stepped foot in it. If a guy worked on Wall Street and lived in New Jersey, the New York State Republican Party considered him its guy and would demand its cut of his donation. It drove Haley up the wall.

To Haley, the New York guys were just bruisers, brass-knuckle types. He didn't like their style. They'd threaten to beat you with a pipe, while Haley would just smile at you—and filet you the second your back was turned.

My loyalty was to Haley. I had a constituency of one. As long as Haley was happy I had no problems. I was working for him for three weeks when I got a pay bump of an additional $10,000 a year because the Midwest field rep had quit and Haley divided up his states and salary among the rest of us rather than bring in someone new. For the first time in my life I was *making* money instead of spending my inheritance.

I was a twenty-nine-year-old newlywed making ninety grand a year, traveling all the time, and seeing my old college buddies all over the Northeast—all thanks to the Gentleman from Mississippi. Whatever the argument, I was on Haley's side. I even started adopting all his prejudices.

Haley didn't like the New York guys? Fuck 'em. I didn't like them, either. I didn't like the way they handled their business and I didn't like the way they had treated me.

Yet the New York Republicans felt about the Southern Strategy the exact way I'd felt just months before under Martini. They had gotten Rudy Giuliani and George Pataki elected without any help from the South. D'Amato had been elected to the Senate before half those Bible thumpers were even in politics. Hell, the Northeastern Republicans had been running the GOP for years before any of the Southern Strategy boys ever showed up. They felt that they'd been fighting the good fight for a long time before anyone had ever heard of Haley Barbour or his pack of drawling yahoos. And, just like that, I was one of the yahoos.

It didn't matter that I was from the Northeast. In politics you're defined by the company you keep. So suddenly, to any moderate East Coast Republican, I represented the Southern Insurgency.

Such regional nuances didn't matter in some of my regions. In West Virginia, for instance, they were just glad I had bothered to show up. The West Virginia state guys were like, "My God! We haven't seen the RNC in forever!"

At a dinner meeting just after that West Virginia trip, I boasted to Haley, "I think we have a very good chance of picking up the governorship of West Virginia."

"And why," said Haley, "would we want that?"

It was a stumper. "Well . . . it's a governorship."

Haley's point was that gaining the West Virginia governorship wouldn't bring the RNC any money or help to maintain the Republican majority in Washington, so what was the value? And governors didn't usually go on to become congressmen or senators because they were already in the most exclusive club in the country—only fifty of them at any given time. I argued that there was intrinsic value in scoring a governor in a Democratic stronghold because it could build momentum that might pay off down the line.

West Virginia would end up being critical to George W. Bush's "win" in the 2000 presidential election, but this was 1996. It was during this time that I had my first face-to-face interaction with "Dubya." That winter, the Republican Governors Association held a meeting at the Renaissance Hotel in D.C. Haley and Ed Gillespie, the RNC's director of communications and congressional affairs, set up a presentation for the governors in the Renaissance's ballroom, which they billed as "The Un-Convention Convention"—to indicate that unconventional things would be discussed.

When Bush saw the "Un-Convention" banner hanging overhead, he put his cowboy boots up on the table, nudged the guy next to him, and said, "U.N.? What's the U.N. got to do with this?" I watched him offer the joke to several different people—sometimes polishing it up with "United Nations" instead of "U.N."—but he never did find any buyers other than his nearby staffers, who were required to laugh.

Getting that close to Bush turned out to be a good thing; if I'd liked the guy, I might have ended up working for him someday. Of all the dubious things I did throughout my career, at least I can honestly say that I did nothing to put George W. Bush in power.

As for West Virginia, Haley didn't care what I did so long as it wasn't going to cost the RNC any money. But of course I wouldn't even have mentioned it if I hadn't intended to hit him up.

David Welch, the media consultant I'd been teamed with on the Corodemus campaign, had been hired to work for the West Virginia State Victory Committee, a front group for wealthy Republicans who were backing Cecil Underwood against Democrat Charlotte Pritt for the governorship in an open race. It seemed far-fetched that a Republican could win, but Welch showed me some polling numbers that implied it was possible. In the first place, state senator Pritt wasn't an incumbent. In the second place, Underwood had something novel going for him; he had already been the governor of West Virginia—from 1957 to 1961. Even back in '57 it had been twenty-four years since a Republican held the office, but still, it wasn't unprecedented.

Welch asked me to get him a little money for some TV spots—only half a million dollars.

As we had learned during the Corodemus run, Welch and I saw eye to eye when it came to opposition research. Digging through Pritt's record, he found that she had cut language requiring background checks for teachers out of a bill going before the state senate. The truth of it was that the West Virginia teachers union didn't want to expose its members to even more bureaucracy for thankless work at miserly wages, and there wasn't a Democrat in the state who could oppose that union and live.

Pritt had also sponsored a bill to have a course on human development and growth taught in public schools, the basic health/sex ed class every middle school kid in America sits through.

Once Welch and I got our hands on these innocent facts, they became the stuff of a thirty-second TV ad that screamed:

"Behind Charlotte Pritt's campaign smile is a liberal voting record she can't hide from. In the state senate, Charlotte Pritt proposed teaching first-graders about condoms. Surprised? You shouldn't be. Senator Pritt also voted to permit the sale of pornographic videos to children. She even voted to allow convicted drug abusers to work in our public schools. . . . Look behind the smile. Charlotte Pritt: Wrong on the issues. Wrong for West Virginia."

All I needed to get the commercial on the air was to find a way to convince Haley Barbour to spend $500,000 on a campaign that couldn't have mattered less to him. As luck would have it, there was a formula.

Federal election laws establish two currencies for political campaigning: hard money and soft. Soft money is unregulated. All the money you raise for the purpose of spending in any election that isn't federal is soft money. Back then, the national committees for both the Democrats and the Republicans were like currency exchanges where people were selling their hard, federal dollars for soft, nonfederal dollars, and vice versa. The law generally held that for every 35 cents of soft money you spent, you could then spend 65 cents on a federal campaign. And it was much easier to raise nonfederal dollars than federal ones.

So if Haley gave me $500,000 to pass on to West Virginia, he was also freeing up roughly $769,200 that the RNC could devote to the federal elections.

Welch got his TV spot, I got the loyalty of a top-notch media consultant who could be a friend down the road, and, in a ma-

jor coming-of-age moment for me as a professional political operative . . . The RNC got slammed with a $10 million libel suit by
Charlotte Pritt.

Cecil Underwood won the election while being able to claim
total ignorance of the ad's origins, because it ended with the line
"Paid for by the West Virginia State Victory Committee," which was
the same kind of state party "victory" organization that had made
Corodemus's life such hell (though it gave him the win). But the fact
is, that ad was bought and paid for entirely with Republican National Committee and National Republican Senatorial Committee
funds. I would know—I delivered the check.

As for Pritt's case, it lingered on for eight years before she finally
lost.

Every election is rigged in one way or another. People have to
pay attention to the way things are couched. They keep saying that
voters are getting more sophisticated every year. They were probably saying the same thing two hundred years ago, yet voters are the
same dupes they've always been. And what is a dupe except someone who lets himself be duped?

It's still only the top-line message that gets through. Everything
else is ignored.

— — —

When Bob Dole secured the presidential nomination at the Republican National Convention in August 1996, the RNC's attention
turned ever so slightly, and truly grudgingly, toward him. We had
all decided way before the convention that Dole had no chance
against Clinton. He may have been a bona fide war hero, but he
also seemed like a mean old man. Not to mention that he had a
twenty-five-year voting record in the Senate in which one could find
an endless supply of things to destroy him with. Clinton and his cronies were going to do the same thing to Dole as we had done to Pritt.
They were going to take any number of perfectly valid votes, define
them in the press, and then leave Dole to explain them. Once a can-

didate has to explain anything that's been defined by his opponent, he's finished.

Very early on in the process, the unspoken secret at the RNC was this: "Forget Dole. He can't win." And he certainly did not have a friend in Haley Barbour. As the Republican nominee, Dole thought it was his right to take over control of the RNC. It might have been, if someone more timid than Haley had been running it. But he was too powerful, too well entrenched, and no one was going to back Dole against him.

Still, it was a fun convention. One night before the nomination was announced, I called an old friend from the convention floor while my states' delegates were going nuts and shouting all around me.

My friend, who was watching the coverage on TV, said, "Dude, it looks crazy there."

"It is!" I replied. "Watch this!"

I started screaming "U-S-A! U-S-A!" and pumping my fist in the air until my whole section picked up the cheer.

"That shit's fucking scary, man!" he yelled into the phone.

"What else do you want them to say?" I asked.

Those TV scenes they show around election time where hordes of citizens spontaneously burst forth with patriotic fervor and zeal for a candidate—they're all orchestrated by guys like me. Sometimes it's to sway the media, sometimes it's just for a laugh. But it's pure theater every time.

One attendee who wasn't buying it was my wife, Elizabeth, who had come out to San Diego for the festivities. On the same day that I'd gotten the crowd to chant for the cameras, Liz and I were walking into the San Diego Convention Center when a news crew stepped up and the female reporter asked if Elizabeth would go on camera for a few questions.

Knowing the minefield it could become, I was shaking my head no at Liz, but she immediately smiled and said, "Of course." The reporter asked if the keynote address by New York congresswoman Susan Molinari the previous evening—it had featured images of her own daughter and her wish that the girl grow up in a world made safer by Bob Dole—had compelled Liz to want to vote for Dole.

Elizabeth looked at the reporter for a moment. Then she said, "Nothing could make me vote for Bob Dole."

I nearly swallowed my tongue. When the reporter asked Elizabeth for her name, I quickly cut in with "Her name is Elizabeth Sherman," using her maiden name as a dodge. Then I grabbed her hand and hustled her off to the convention floor.

The convention for the "family values" Party was, in the end, really just a sweaty, slippery boozefest that put some of your less temperate frats to shame. Walking back to my hotel after the "Melee for Haley" fund-raiser, I found one of my esteemed colleagues facedown in a puddle of mud. This guy was forty-five years old and the mud was literally bubbling around his face because the son of a bitch was drowning in it. I picked him up, strapped him to a golf cart where the clubs belonged, and drove what was left of him right into the lobby of his hotel. Ah, to be the cream of the crop in American politics.

After the convention, I arranged a Pennsylvania fly-around for Haley that included a press event in Lancaster County, a very Republican-friendly area in a state where Dole needed an extremely high turnout among the faithful if he was to have a chance of winning its electoral votes. None were more faithful to Dole than senior citizens in Lancaster County.

It was just Haley and me in the 84 Lumber private jet, heading for Pennsylvania, when he turned to me and said, "Why are we doing this event?"

"Well, the press you get will help with turnout, and Dole needs the turnout."

"Well, it better work," he countered. "Your job is on the line."

Well, fuck, I thought—that's the kind of thing you could've told me before I set this thing up! I didn't know whether Haley was screwing with me or if my ass was really on the line. Since Haley wasn't going to tell me, I felt the safest bet was to assume the latter.

It turned out to be a very hot day, so hot that none of the 350 seniors who showed up at the open-air event would sit in the chairs in front of the stage. The sun was too strong. To a casual observer—and there are no observers more casually lazy than the press—it looked as if no one had shown up to hear Haley speak because all those weary Methuselahs were staying in the shade of the trees.

I kept telling the reporters, "Don't pay attention to the empty chairs! They're in the trees! The old people are in the trees! The old people are in the trees!"

For reasons unknown, Haley didn't fire me. And the newspaper clips the next day validated the event.

At another Pennsylvania event, this time featuring Dole, I was standing with some of his advance people watching him wave to the crowd as he headed for his four-car motorcade. Just as Dole was climbing in, some dumbass kid in RollerBlades and no shirt came flying around the corner screaming, "I'm Bob Dole! I'm Bob Dole!"

Before you knew it, ten Secret Service guys were on top of him—one literally standing on the kid's head—with guns drawn. Every car in the motorcade suddenly revealed an arsenal. I swear I saw a Gatling gun sticking out of one of them.

With one Secret Service agent screaming, "Go! Go! Go!" they tossed Dole into his vehicle like a sack and peeled out.

The next thing I set up for Haley was a meeting with John Rollins, an enormously wealthy businessman and former lieutenant governor of Delaware. I remember that the guy had his own helipad on the roof of his luxury office building outside of Wilmington. Rollins was a member of "Team 100," which meant that he had already donated $100,000 to the Party at some point. Now Haley was going to touch him for another hundred grand.

I was excited to watch Haley do it. I'd never seen anyone ask anyone for that kind of money before. How do you ask a person for $100,000?

We went up to Rollins's office, Haley made some small talk, and, with the niceties out of the way, he leaned toward the guy. "I understand you might be willing to give a hundred thousand dollars to the RNC."

"Yes," he said. "I want to make sure some of that money goes back to Delaware, but I'm willing to do it."

At that, Haley leaned in closer and told him, "Well, that's great. A hundred thousand dollars is tremendous, and we'll definitely make sure that a portion of that goes back to the state committee. But what I *really* need from you, what you could *really* do to help your country . . . I need two hundred thousand dollars."

The room went silent as Rollins thought it over.

"Can some of that money go to Delaware, too?"

"Absolutely!"

"Okay, I'm in."

It blew my mind. Haley just upped the ante from a sure $100,000 to double that in about sixty seconds. It was fucking amazing. I'd have taken the $100,000 and gotten the hell out of there before Rollins changed his mind. Lesson learned, Mr. Barbour.

At the end of September, when Bob Dole fell off a stage at a campaign rally in Chico, California, the RNC just cut him off. It was more important to keep the Republican majorities. At the dinner meeting, Haley told us, "Well, boys, I think we need to concentrate on the House and the Senate. Senator Dole, we need to help him fight the good fight, but we also need to protect our majorities." From now on, all RNC money would be going toward the House and Senate contests, with not another cent being wasted on a doomed presidential bid.

After that, guys like me who could have spent time on the Dole campaign just didn't. We paid it no attention. We even stopped taking calls from the Dole camp. Even Dole's own staff was distancing itself from him.

His chief advance guy was Keith Nahigian—who had previously distinguished himself by misspelling *potato* on cue cards he prepared for Dan Quayle before the infamous 1992 Trenton elementary school photo op where the vice president informed a sixth-grader, "You're close, but you left a little something off. The 'e' on the end."

The week after Dole's tumble in Chico, I stopped by Keith's office at campaign headquarters in Washington, D.C., near Union Station. In Keith's office I saw, prominently displayed behind his desk, the length of white picket fence railing that had broken and caused Dole to fall. The historic humiliation of his candidate provided a nifty little memento for Keith.

Cynic or not, I at least believed that you needed to care about your candidate. I have to admit, though, that when Dole fell off that stage my first reaction was "Damn, he still managed to hold on to that pen." Then again, I worked for the RNC, not Dole. Dole's people just wanted to follow him to the White House to fulfill God knew what ambitions. During the race, one of his fund-raising guys, Mark Miller, had actually said to me, "Once I'm in the White House, I can get even with everyone."

Mark never made it to the White House, but others of his species had only to wait four years.

Dole and his people were out of business, but the business of Haley Barbour and the RNC had never been better. I had made a lot of solid new contacts, filled out my Rolodex, and was a young man in good standing with one of the most powerful players in the country. I was gaining the experience that I hoped would propel me to the top echelon of professional campaign runners. I was one step closer to the ultimate prize: managing a competitive presidential campaign.

EIGHT

One of the people whose wild aspirations died with the Dole campaign was Julie Finley, a millionaire widow who was among the most prominent of Washington's Ladies Who Lunch—the blue-haired socialite fund-raisers from whose galas flowed the lifeblood of the D.C. Republican Party. Most of them were satisfied with having a say over the business of the D.C. Party, which is about as useful an apparatus as a watercooler at the bottom of a lake. Finley, however, had been a major donor for Dole and had expected to be paid back with an ambassadorship or some such bagatelle when he took office. Now that that was over, she decided that she should be the cochairman of the RNC.

The title of cochairman is a misnomer, since the RNC's cochairman is subordinate rather than equal to the chairman. Julie Finley filling the position was only one prospective outcome of the coming RNC elections of 1997 that I didn't look forward to. Haley Barbour was stepping down and it would hardly matter who ended up replacing him—whoever it was, he would be no Haley Barbour.

Haley had taken the reins in 1993, orchestrated the Republican takeover, saw the Party lose consecutive presidential elections, and decided he'd done enough. His lobbying firm was already set up and waiting for him by the time Dole went down, and now he was going over to K Street to make a boatload of money.

So while Julie Finley was mounting her campaign, I was looking for new opportunities.

Though Finley was one of the 165 voting members of the RNC, and though her D.C. stomping ground was one of my RNC territories, she had no use for me. It was all very mutual. Finley had no use for me because the RNC would never throw away money on her pet causes.

An author, entrepreneur, and lobbyist named Patricia Harrison was considering running against Finley for the cochair spot. We had a mutual friend in Karl Saliba, who had worked with me at the RNC and was now in the same lobbyist circles as Harrison. Karl introduced us, thinking I might be able to help with her campaign.

She was accomplished, vivacious, attractive, stylish, and a shrewd businesswoman. She would be a breath of fresh air for the RNC.

I told her, "You can't win."

Pat's problem was that the RNC was a better fit for an oxygen mask than a breath of fresh air. She wasn't a Washington insider, although she had some George H. W. Bush bona fides. There was no cheap little elephant pinned to her lapel. Pat wasn't even a voting member of the RNC. She had no constituency.

"I want to run for change," she said. "The fact that we lost to Bill Clinton again only proves that the Party is going in the wrong direction."

It was all blah-blah-blah to me. If she had said she was a rabid pro-lifer, I'd have said, "Show up with a fetus in a jar and you might stand a chance."

For all the chatter it had made during the '94 Revolution, the Republican Party's whole job is to lumber on maintaining the status quo of, say, 1956. Its mission is *not* to change. Why do you think they call it the Establishment?

But Pat had already made up her mind, and with Haley on the

way out I needed to drum up some options as to what I'd do next. I wanted every friend in Washington I could get. RNC headquarters was in D.C., D.C. was one of my territories, and once you acquire a taste for D.C., you can't go back to provincial fare.

I couldn't technically work for her without quitting my job, and I wasn't ready to do that yet, but I agreed to help her. She couldn't have paid me anyway; her campaign didn't have any money—it didn't have anything. Well, it did have ideas. So it's like I said.

"If you help me," she asked, "what are you going to want in return?"

"When the time comes, I'll let you know."

I tapped Blaise Lewis, a very talented operative I knew from the RNC as Curt Anderson's protégé, to manage the campaign. Karl Saliba and I stayed on as unofficial consultants. It was late November of 1996 and the RNC elections were in January 1997. Pat started flying around the country, meeting the voting members and trying to build an organization. She was as pro-choice as you could get, but she played it coy on abortion, never taking a position. Instead, she talked about what the RNC could do if it were wrested away from the old guard. It was hard going, but she began to tap into something.

Even though the 165 members of the RNC were part of the Establishment, they were also working people with lives and thoughts of their own. They were a little sick of a tiny clique of Washington insiders telling them who their leadership was going to be and how they should vote. They were a little sick of the Julie Finleys of the world.

When the 165 voting members of the RNC converged on the Renaissance Hotel for the winter meeting, at which the elections would be held, Pat was doing better than I'd expected. A little less than a third of the committee had pledged their support for her. But obviously it wasn't good enough. Unless we found something to knock Finley out of the lead, Pat was going to lose in the morning.

One thing we knew about Julie Finley was that she was a prolific fund-raiser; she gave a lot of money to a lot of Republicans. Well, who were all these people? Perhaps some of them were Republicans who didn't fully represent all the ideals of the Grand Old Party. We did a search of the FEC database where all contributions and disbursements are recorded. When the data came back, one name stood out like a stain on one of Finley's ball gowns: Harvey Gantt.

Not only was Harvey Gantt a Democrat, not only was Harvey Gantt a black Democrat, he was a black Democrat civil rights hero who had twice run and lost against Jesse Helms for the U.S. Senate in North Carolina. Now, he must sound like a good man, and donating money to his campaign against the much-reviled Jesse Helms must sound to most rational people like a good thing to do. But, despite all its spin, you have to remember that the Republican Party has two main characteristics:

It is white, and to the right.

And I'm not talking about the 1920s, or the 1950s, or even the 1980s. A week before the 1990 Election Day showdown between Helms and Gantt—who in 1963 became the first African-American ever to attend Clemson University in South Carolina—Republican strategist Alex Castellanos created a thirty-second TV spot over the course of a weekend. It was called "Hands."

A pair of white hands is seen crumpling a job rejection letter. The accompanying voiceover says, "You needed that job. You were the best qualified. But they had to give it to a minority because of a racial quota. Is that really fair? Harvey Gantt says it is. Harvey Gantt supports Ted Kennedy's racial quota law that makes the color of your skin more important than your qualifications. You vote on this issue next Tuesday. For racial quotas: Harvey Gantt. *Against* racial quotas: Jesse Helms."

Of course, it's impossible to name an American who more fervently supported treating one race differently from another than Jesse Helms did. But that homegrown police chief's son who never earned a degree in his life was the darling of the Religious Right and the very personification of what the average pissed-off Republican white guy believed. That Julie Finley had given his opponent $2,000 would be seen as utter heresy. And we had it right there on paper.

The only problem was how to get the information to the membership. Once it was out there, Pat needed to have plausible deniability as to its origins so that she could lie and look convincing doing it. We divorced her from the process. If this had been a regular election, she could have shouted that contribution from the rafters. But RNC elections were supposed to be about courtesy among a unified group of friends. There was no room for personal attacks, no slash and burn. These were cordial, genteel affairs, conducted with all the dignity of a solemn family ceremony.

We decided we'd slip the documents under everyone's doors while they were sleeping.

It was simple enough. All the members were staying at the Renaissance and we had their room numbers. We made 165 copies of the FEC report, highlighted the Gantt contribution, and Blaise Lewis took over from there for a middle-of-the-night distribution. It would be the first thing the members saw the morning of the vote.

We sat back and waited for morning.

The anonymous under-the-door delivery was nothing new, by the way. The notorious 1988 Michael Dukakis tank ad that made the Democratic presidential nominee look like Snoopy on his doghouse fighter plane was the result of just such a surreptitious drop. Greg Stevens, who produced the ad, told my classmates and me all about it when he lectured at the GSPM. The footage used in the Bush/Quayle ad attacking Dukakis's record on national defense was from a photo op arranged by the Dukakis campaign to which only the press had been invited. It shows Dukakis sitting atop an M1 Abrams tank in tanker headgear with the knot of his tie tufting out of a military jumpsuit. No one in the GOP had any access to the embarrassing footage. In fact, no one in the Party even knew it existed, until someone anonymously—and literally—slipped it into Stevens's office.

Obviously, Stevens would have been a fool not to use the material, but the fact that he ever got his hands on it speaks to dirty pool by a member of the supposedly "unbiased" news media. The spot, which followed the Willie Horton furlough attack ad on Dukakis, sealed the 1988 Democratic nominee's fate at the polls.

The first event of the day consisted of regional breakfasts. The RNC members were arranged in different conference rooms according to where they hailed from, and the candidates would circulate among them giving speeches to rally their supporters and win over any of the undecided.

As luck would have it, Finley's first meeting was with the Southern region, Jesse Helms's backyard. All the Southerners started giving Finley dirty looks and she had no idea why, since they'd already pledged her their support. It was as if she had ten feet of toilet paper stuck to her heel and everyone saw it but her.

Just as she was starting to give her stump speech, someone raised his hand and said, "We appreciate all that, Julie, but can you please explain your contribution to Harvey Gantt?"

"What are you talking about? I never gave money to Harvey Gantt."

He took the paper out and handed it to her, saying, "Well, according to the FEC, you did. And here it is."

It was a total kick in the gut, but she took it in stride at first. "Well, I make a lot of contributions. I don't recall that particular one."

As more people began demanding answers, panic set in. Finley had never lived through a real campaign, had never been opposed, had never seen adversity of any sort in her political life. To her the whole race had been merely a predetermined exercise: she was going to win, bring all her pals from the Dole campaign into the RNC leadership, and it would all be good times again.

As Finley progressed from one regional breakfast to the next, the Gantt contribution followed her like a stink. She couldn't escape it and she couldn't mollify her RNC colleagues who were appalled at the idea of electing a cochairman of the Republican National Committee who was not pure in her Republican convictions. The first time something didn't go the way she expected it to, she totally fell apart. By the time she got to the last regional breakfast she decided to go with the worst excuse possible, telling the RNC members through choked-back tears, "My husband was dying of brain cancer and he asked me to make the contribution. It was his dying wish!"

Fortunately for Finley, the regional meetings ended before she could say much more. Everyone moved down to the basement ballroom where the elections would be held. Pat wasn't allowed on the floor because she wasn't a voting member, so I went down to serve as her eyes and ears—as well as to do my actual job as an RNC employee, which that day consisted of gathering up all the votes from my regions while working the convention floor.

With the first ballot cast, no one had a clear majority, but Pat had a little more than a third of the vote. While the mood had soured against Finley, a lot of members still didn't want Pat because she was an outsider. When the second ballot was cast, the only result was that it eliminated a third candidate who had never had a chance in the first place. It was going to come down to a third-ballot runoff between Pat and Finley.

At that point some of the members started going crazy. They didn't want a runoff. Pat was simply unacceptable because she didn't owe them anything. They didn't know her and they had nothing to control her with—no carrot, no stick. But with the Gantt revelation, Finley was not an acceptable alternative.

A motion was made from the floor to allow a new candidate to enter the race. They wanted to enter Betsy deVos, of the Amway and Prince Corporation fortunes, an RNC member from Michigan.

"We're drafting her!" someone yelled from the floor, which led to a lot of parliamentary maneuvering on all sides. Finally, it was ruled from the dais that the deVos party was shit out of luck, which didn't really matter because Betsy deVos, to her credit, addressed the RNC members, telling them that under no circumstances would she accept the position, since she was not a candidate.

On the third ballot, Pat won overwhelmingly.

I remember I just stood there smiling to myself and thinking, I just hijacked the Republican National Committee—that's pretty cool.

Now I had a legitimate claim to the RNC; I had total access to its cochair, my client.

Just then, I heard from across the room the kind of wailing that's normally reserved for a funeral or a fatal diagnosis. Julie Finley had grabbed her things and was running crying from the room. Good, I thought, don't forget your Fendi purse, Julie!

That's why she deserved to lose. If you're going to cry when you lose, how can you run the RNC? How can you run any adult organization? You take your lumps and you keep on fighting, but you don't cry about it. Not ever.

There's no crying in politics.

NINE

Once the buzz of the win wore off, it felt a little like a hollow victory because I frankly had a fair amount of disdain for the position of RNC cochairman. Politically speaking, landing that job is akin to declaring, "Look what I didn't step in!" It wasn't a bad thing to have a good relationship with the RNC's number two, but despite my earlier high, there wasn't any real power there.

Pat offered me her chief of staff position and I declined it immediately. It was January 1997, and my idea was to find a Senate or gubernatorial race to manage so that within the next year or so I'd gain the clout to get a top position on a presidential campaign for the 2000 election. But '97 was an off year in the election cycle and there were very few campaign jobs to be found. So, after a month of Pat pecking me on the head, I took the chief of staff job with the proviso that I'd be out within a year.

The only thing about that year that wasn't completely mind-numbing was that it gave me the opportunity to teach at the RNC's campaign management colleges.

The "colleges" are three-day intensive courses held in hotels all over the country about six times a year. They're intended to teach budding and would-be political professionals how campaigns are run in the real world, rather than in a college lecture hall. I went through one myself in grad school. A typical syllabus would make it all seem innocuous enough: how to draw up an earned media plan ("earned" meaning that your candidate did something to merit press attention without your having to buy it); how to use paid media; and how to write a press release and organize volunteers. But "how to" contains multitudes of permutations.

I would go in and cherry-pick a topic I wanted to talk about and tell the kids what I thought they needed to hear. The RNC brought me its next generation of press secretaries, campaign managers, and political directors, and I taught them all the great things I'd learned during my five years in politics—namely, how to use phones, direct mail, and the press to reconstruct reality to your own specifications. I happily taught eager young souls how to, for lack of a better phrase, corrupt the system. Or was I teaching them that the system is corrupt and that they'd better learn how to use it to their advantage? Semantics.

By 1998 I was desperate to get out of Pat's office. It was an okay place to hang your hat for a few months, but a career it didn't make. I also didn't have a lot of confidence in the RNC's new chairman.

Haley's successor was an RNC member from Colorado named Jim Nicholson. Nicholson was a nice enough guy, a former army ranger and successful businessman who went on to become the U.S. ambassador to the Vatican and secretary of veterans affairs for President Bush, No. 43. Following Haley Barbour is unfair to anybody. But my opinion of Nicholson took a considerable hit at our first meeting, when he scribbled a note asking for more information on "ICED TEA." I thought to myself, Snapple? Later that day it hit me like a shot—ISTEA, the Intermodal Surface Transportation Efficiency Act, pronounced "ice tea." I knew this because my former boss Martini sat on the House Transportation Committee. Jim Nicholson was a sharp enough politician, but he was no Haley Barbour. If Haley ever slipped up, no one ever saw him do it.

Fortunately for me, the Republicans were desperate to fend off any Democratic attack on their Senate majority in the coming election and they needed a few seasoned operatives for the task.

My old RNC boss Curt Anderson called me up and said, "Why don't you come over to the Senate committee and work with Dave Hanson on some Senate races? It would be good for your career and you'd get to work at a pretty high level. We want you over here." He sealed the offer with this ringing endorsement: "We think you're competent."

The National Republican Senatorial Committee (NRSC), to which Curt was referring, is the GOP's campaign arm charged with electing Republicans to the Senate. The Dave Hanson whom Curt mentioned had been the RNC field rep for the mountain states when I was covering the mid-Atlantic; now he was the NRSC's political director. I'd never gotten very cozy with Hanson—he was in his fifties and, well, he was from the mountain states—but I wasn't going to let that get in the way of a sweet position rubbing elbows with powerful senatorial contenders all over the country.

The chance to gain real hands-on experience in Senate campaigns was a huge deal. Senate races exist above the clouds. Unlike a House race, you don't have to scramble in the dirt for every nickel and tiny bit of press. Senate candidates usually come with a vast supply of money, and they always come with an endless amount of press. Since there are only one hundred senators at any one time, your candidate will get press every time he or she steps out of a car, and not just in the papers, but on TV—where the news is such a frenzy of color and noise that there's never any danger of the truth upstaging the political message.

Once you've gotten yourself a prime-time candidate, you can twist, spin, and contort reality until the reporters, the voters, and even you can't look at the Frankenstein thing you've created and say with any certainty what the hell it is.

There was only one obstacle between that job and me, and he was formidable.

Kentucky senior senator Mitch McConnell had just been elected chairman of the NRSC. He was a champion earner for the GOP; his rabid opposition to any and all campaign finance reform was the stuff of legend. He was also a scary, scary man.

I was summoned to an interview with McConnell at the Russell Senate Office Building. When I was shown into the senator's office, he was sitting on a couch reading what looked like a memo. He did not look up at me. His assistant ushered me to the sofa opposite McConnell and I sat down. The senator still did not look up at me. After about two minutes, McConnell decided to cast me a glance. Then he didn't say anything. He went on reading in silence for literally another three minutes, killing me.

It got to a point where I was either going to break the ice myself or jump out the fucking window, regardless of elevation. So I offered "I'm very eager to work for you at the Senatorial Committee."

"Well," he said, "okay."

He might have said fifteen words during the entire interview. He asked me what impression I had gotten of the RNC when I'd been a field rep and what my campaign experience had been in general. Much like my initial RNC interview with Curt Anderson, everything I said met a dead silence, minus the lip-popping I'd become accustomed to with Curt. Senator McConnell let that silence hang there and hang there so that I was forced to elaborate on everything I said until either I'd finally told him something interesting or proved myself a total fool.

At the end of twenty minutes, McConnell said, "Well, thanks for coming by," and returned to his reading. I walked out of there in a sweat, with no idea what had just happened.

Dave Hanson called a few hours later. "Welcome on board," he said. "I hear the meeting went really well with the senator."

What, I wondered, would a bad meeting have involved? Rusty hooks and a ball gag? I was relieved that the senator approved of me, but I never wanted to be alone with him again. He terrified me. With Haley Barbour, you always knew he was serious and that you had to do a good job, but he was also open and gregarious. Senator McConnell was like a sheet of drywall. He could probably sit straight-backed and rigid for seventy-two hours without a bathroom break if he needed to. As I said, terrifying, but it's also what made him a great politician. Forget never letting anyone see you sweat—McConnell wouldn't let you see him breathe.

And he didn't expect his employees to go around breathing easy, either. I'd barely started working for McConnell when he called Dave Hanson and me into his office to give him the latest update on our races. When Dave finished speaking, the senator said, "Can you tell me anything that's *not* in the Hotline today?"

The Hotline was *Congressional Quarterly*'s daily rundown of all the political news being reported in the papers that day. Dave had been nailed. He responded like a true politico; he passed the nailing down to me.

"Allen," he said, "why don't you answer that question?"

I was good in those situations. What makes a successful candidate is the same thing that makes a successful campaigner—anything you say is true if you say it with enough authority. So, as usual, I took some random gossip I'd heard God knew where about the embattled Illinois Democratic senator Carol Moseley-Braun and her alleged ties to a Nigerian dictator, padded it out with conjecture, numbers, and hyperbole, and got us out of that office with our asses intact.

I chose three races to focus on in that cycle—a surefire win in Illinois, a guaranteed loss in Vermont, and a toss-up in Wisconsin.

My favorite campaign was in Vermont, despite our candidate having no chance there. Jack McMullen was running against Democratic incumbent Patrick Leahy. Vermont would sooner elect a doorknob or an old pair of gloves to the Senate than replace Leahy, but McMullen was a self-funder and I really liked the guy so I put a lot of time into his campaign.

The NRSC's main target, however, was Senator Moseley-Braun

of Illinois. Moseley-Braun, the only African-American woman ever elected to the U.S. Senate, topped the hit list because her first term in office had been a cavalcade of scandals. Most of them revolved around her Nigerian boyfriend and her questionably financed trips to Nigeria. Whoever the Republican was who got the nomination to run against Moseley-Braun, he or she was pretty much guaranteed to become a U.S. senator.

Peter Fitzgerald was the scion of a Chicago banking family who had served in the state legislature and had run for the House and lost. He was the biggest self-funder running. Because he was financially self-sufficient, I got the sense that he didn't care about building a coalition. He was that rare candidate who didn't have to rely on anyone or return favors. For the Party, having such a Republican in the Senate was only slightly more appealing than having a Democrat in the seat. So Fitzgerald didn't have much institutional support, but he had more money than any other Republican candidate in Illinois, and he did win the nomination.

When Fitzgerald got the nod, McConnell informed me, "I'm not giving any money to Peter Fitzgerald. He's got his own money. Now go tell him."

Hey, super! Thanks, Mitch! Our candidate, the next junior senator from the great state of Illinois, would now have no use for me. But I wanted to have something to offer if not cash when I got to Chicago, so I put together a direct mail packet to pitch to his campaign. At the boardroom of Fitzgerald's bank, which he was using as his campaign office, I held off delivering the bad news and made small talk with the candidate and his advisors.

"I put together a direct mail program," I told them, "just as a sample for you guys to take a look at and consider as you're planning for your campaign in the fall."

What I didn't know was that they had already hired the king of direct mail smear campaigns, Karl Rove. As if guided by the same primordial, threat-sensing ESP that sends animals running for high ground before the rain ever comes, Rove came slouching into the boardroom almost as soon as I took the packet from my briefcase.

He didn't introduce himself, just sat down and put his laptop on the desk.

"Allen," Fitzgerald said, "do you know Karl Rove?"

"Oh, it's nice to meet you."

Rove cut off the introductions with "What's that?" and gestured at the packet.

"This is a sample direct mail plan that Allen just gave us."

Rove took it, looked it over, then flipped open his laptop and went to work in a quiet fury. I figured he just wasn't paying attention and so I went on discussing direct mail with the rest of the group. Even as I remained calm and professional, the old adage "If you don't know who the sucker in the room is, it's you" popped into my head.

For fifteen minutes we were going back and forth about my mail plan while all Fitzgerald wanted to know was "Am I getting my co-ordinated from Senator McConnell?"—by which he meant his matching funds from the Republican Senatorial Committee. I still wasn't ready to tell him, because once I did he would show me the door and I still thought there must be something I could do for his campaign. He was going to win and I wanted to be on the team one way or another.

All of a sudden, Rove cut in again, saying, "How about a direct mail plan that's something like this?" He whipped his laptop around and showed it to the table. "I was thinking we'd do something more along these lines," he told the group—while picking up my meticu-lous little packet and folding it into his coat pocket. He disappeared the thing like it was a witness at a mob trial—or the transcript of a Dick Cheney energy task force meeting.

The mail was how Rove made his money. He was likely getting at least a 15 percent cut of any money he arranged to have Fitzgerald spend on direct mail and he wasn't about to let me walk in and slip out with his meal ticket. And that year Fitzgerald was spending $14 million of his own money to beat the incumbent. The message was lost on no one, because when Rove "suggested" his own mail strategy, the tone was clearly "This is the plan; I don't know who you are, but shut the fuck up and get out of here."

Hey, it was time to go. I ran my ass back to O'Hare Airport and I still hadn't told Fitzgerald that he wasn't getting his coordinated funding from the committee. On the flight back to D.C. all I thought about was how to get Fitzgerald that money. The answer was an old standby: soft money.

I made my proposition in the Senatorial Committee's ceremonial chairman's office, a ponderous room with about a mile and a half of thick drapery and a prodigious desk that never had any paperwork on it because no one ever used it.

"I know you don't want to give any coordinated money to Peter Fitzgerald," I told McConnell, "but how about eight hundred thousand dollars in corporate money? If you move that over to the state Party that'll help them in their turnout efforts for Peter. So you're not directly helping Peter, you're not giving up any of the federal money, but you can legitimately go to him after he wins and tell him you put eight hundred thousand dollars into the race."

"That's a great idea," he said. "Let's do that."

It felt pretty good to make a deal for eight hundred grand. And it was the only way to get in tight with the state Party ops in Illinois. Going back to Chicago with an $800,000 check, I could meet anyone I wanted to. It was essentially the same game as bringing the five-grand "cover charge" to get in the door with the New York State GOP guys in Albany, but the numbers were much bigger and the stakes were going up. Bottom line: I was widening my network and increasing my political worth. For anyone in my position, that was what mattered.

In any campaign, the people behind the scenes are asking themselves, "How does this benefit me specifically?" Anyone who says differently is full of shit. In politics, the second you stop looking for every opportunity to make contacts—and to bring those contacts money—you're dead.

No Senate race that year held McConnell's personal attention like Feingold versus Neumann in Wisconsin. Russ Feingold was the freshman Democratic senator and Mark Neumann was the Republican House member challenging him. In his first term, Feingold had set himself up as the Senate's premier proponent of campaign finance reform; McConnell was the chief proponent of the status quo. McConnell had cobbled together a strange coalition of some of the most liberal and most conservative groups in the country to oppose Feingold's reform movement, but that movement struck a chord with voters that went beyond party lines. McConnell badly needed Feingold out of office.

I set up a fly-around of Wisconsin for McConnell to put the touch on various donors around the state. It had been a raging success, bringing in half a million dollars in one day for the NRSC that could be earmarked for Mark Neumann, but McConnell still had a talent for scaring me half shitless. Now I was stuck in a twin-engine plane with the guy just inches from me at twelve thousand feet. In such close quarters the desire for conversation is, well, considerable, but McConnell's no talker. He sat there reading the whole time. The last leg of the fly-around brought us to La Crosse, Wisconsin, from where I was going to fly to Milwaukee and then on to Vermont to check in on the grand quixotic adventure that was the McMullen campaign.

When I said good-bye to the senator and checked in at the tiny airport for my connecting flight, the Northwest Airlines attendant informed me that all commercial flights for the next three days had been canceled because of an airline strike.

Looking out at the tarmac, I could still see McConnell's little private plane puttering around the runway and waiting for its turn to take off.

"I just got off that plane. I've got to get back on that plane!"

Clearly it was a flyspeck of an airport because the attendant actually got on the phone with the tower and had them hold the plane for me.

I watched the plane come to a halt and, once again—terror. Did I really just keep Old Drywall's plane from taking off? Out on the tarmac, the door opened and the stairs dropped down and I climbed aboard while avoiding McConnell's stare.

"You know," he said, "a lesser man would've thrown in the towel."

From there, he suddenly opened up. There was one other person on the plane, Steven Law, a longtime McConnell aide who was the executive director at the NRSC. McConnell told us this story about another fly-around, in Kentucky, where a young volunteer had accompanied him part of the way. The kid drove him to the airport and, as the plane took off, McConnell saw him running alongside it and waving to him.

He had turned to the person next to him and said, "What a nice guy! Look at him waving at me!" The senator remembered, "I waved back to that young man. Half an hour later, I realized I was sitting on his car keys!"

Everyone on the plane was in tears. The joke itself may not have merited it, but we were all laughing hard because it was so out of character for the senator.

By the summer of 1998 my professional life was everything I had wanted it to be at that point. I was a key player in three senatorial campaigns, and by the time the elections rolled around in November I'd be in a prime position to snag my coveted presidential campaign. Elizabeth was not impressed.

Our first son, Sam, was born at 7:35 on a July morning. An

hour later, I had a previously scheduled conference call with Jack McMullen in Vermont and a pollster named Jim McLaughlin. Elizabeth was in bed, exhausted but elated, holding our first child. I wasn't nearly as tired, but equally elated.

Glancing at my watch I said to Elizabeth, "I have a conference call."

She gave me the look of death and said, "You have got to be kidding me."

I gave her the "What can I do?" face, shrugged, and said, "I'll make it quick."

McLaughlin proceeded to go into an in-depth explanation about the data from the latest survey. I played along for a while but finally broke under Elizabeth's stare, telling my conference call pals, "I have to go, guys. My son was just born."

After a pause, McMullen said, "Why are you even on this call? Go! And congratulations!" McLaughlin said the same thing. When I hung up, I got another look from Elizabeth; this one said she'd just developed a grudge she would hang on to forever.

I was a total ass!

And there was plenty of it to go around.

In Madison, Wisconsin, Feingold nailed Mark Neumann royally. Feingold and Neumann were going to have a debate in which the questions came from an audience of prescreened voters. Before the debate, R. J. Johnson, Neumann's campaign manager, pointed to a college girl in the audience and told Neumann, "Just be aware that that girl over there is a volunteer for the Feingold campaign. So if she asks a question, you know it's not going to be friendly."

Neumann said, "That's good to know. Thanks."

Nothing could have been worse to know.

The debate was the usual platitudes until the Feingold girl finally stood up and asked Neumann a question that was clearly designed to make him look like a knuckle-dragger who wanted nothing less than to strip the earth of its essential parts and sell them for scrap at a discount.

As soon as Neumann stood up, I thought, R.J. probably shouldn't have told him she works for Feingold.

Neumann had this for an opener: "First let me say, that's a loaded question." He followed up with "I know for a fact that you're a volunteer on the Feingold campaign."

He may as well have brought some orphans to kick around the stage. The girl burst into tears. "No I'm not!" she sobbed. "I'm just here to participate in democracy!"

Here was a nineteen-year-old girl who was at a Senate debate instead of getting tattooed and chugging forties outside a 7-Eleven, and there was the bastard who made her cry. He was no longer just a suspected Neanderthal; he was a confirmed Neanderthal who'd just clubbed a girl over the head. There is no way to spin that. You can shoot as many old men in the face as you like, but make one girl cry . . . After that, you can have six daughters show up and say how great you are; half the voters won't hear it and the other half will think you forced them to do it at the end of a belt.

Neumann of course did everything he could to spin it, saying that while he was sorry if he hurt her feelings, a campaign volunteer didn't belong at the debate. Everything he said just made him seem like more of a jerk.

Whether the Feingold camp had staged the crying or if the girl had just been really nervous about attending a debate in civilian disguise, it was genius. All you saw on the news that night was that girl crying. All of Neumann's carefully crafted answers were out the window. That's how fast it can happen. The race was over.

Despite Neumann's misfortune, working on Senate campaigns was the best thing I could have done during the 1998 elections. If nothing else, it allowed me to ignore all the Monica Lewinsky sex scandal dogma the GOP had been spewing since January. That stuff was interesting as gossip when it started, but when the guys in the House began calling for Clinton's impeachment I thought they'd all gone nuts. Few Senate candidates were using "Interngate" as part of their platform, so it was just background noise to me, but that noise still didn't make any sense.

For one thing, no survey data I'd looked at gave the Republicans any chance of gaining the sixty-seven-seat supermajority in the senate that it would take to impeach Clinton. And even if they could get those numbers, why would they get rid of Clinton just to have Al Gore take over the office? The only thing an impeachment would accomplish would be to make Gore the incumbent in the 2000 presidential contest, practically guaranteeing his election to the White House.

To me, it was all just hate-based nonsense from the Southern Strategy in the House. And leading the way was Representative Bob Barr of Georgia, who spent as much time playing down his connection to the racist Council of Conservative Citizens as he did frothing at the mouth about Clinton's hummer perjury. A backwoods knucklehead was using sex to become the face of the Republican Party. Granted there was a principled case to be made about perjury, but the last time the House GOP spun its wheels on principle was during the 1995 budget crisis, which ended up shutting down the government.

That was some strategy, that Southern Strategy!

On election night I was at NRSC headquarters counting returns. The Fitzgerald win and the McMullen loss had been presupposed for months, so all McConnell cared about that evening was Feingold versus Neumann in Wisconsin. As more and more votes came in, it was close, but clear that Neumann had bitten it and that McConnell's nemesis could go on hounding him around D.C. for another six years.

I was about ready to go home when McConnell stopped by.

"Well," he said, "it looks like you lost." With that, he left the room.

I never saw him again.

Curt Anderson must have really liked me because the guy couldn't stop giving me work. After the '98 election cycle Steve Forbes hired Curt as a consultant on his campaign for the Republican presidential nomination and Curt asked if I wanted in.

Did I! Finally, a presidential bid! This was it. Everything was going according to plan. The only thing I didn't account for was Steve Forbes.

I initially thought that Forbes could be a contender because he had money, a personal fortune of half a billion dollars. When Forbes ran in the '96 GOP primaries he had caused Bob Dole serious trouble by attacking him on his long public record of tax increases and special-interest ties, using hard-hitting television ads in early primary states such as Iowa, New Hampshire, and Arizona. At the same time, Forbes had made headlines and attracted followers with his proposal for a flat tax. But for all that, the guy looked like he'd been put together on an operating table. He had a stammering speech pattern that made you think he was on the verge of a seizure with each tortured sentence, and he seemed generally uncomfortable in his own skin. You might be able to sell that in a congressional race, but a president has to have either charisma or the ability to fake it.

Yet I liked the idea that voters might go for having a thinker in the Oval Office for a change. Steve Forbes may have been a pensive nerd, but the American people had been sold on intellectuals before. Abraham Lincoln came to mind—no offense to Lincoln. And with competition like a Connecticut-raised cowboy who'd been blind drunk until he was forty and who'd failed at every private-sector job his father ever got him, I thought Forbes could really have a shot if he spent his money wisely. Conveniently, I set aside the fact that Forbes's own daddy had gotten him his job.

Forbes's campaign manager, Bill Dal Col—a close advisor and confidant of the candidate's who actually lived on the Forbes family compound in Bedminster, New Jersey—hired me on as a consultant and gave me the title of deputy political director. Who was the political director? Jim Tobin, my old friend from the RNC.

One of my first assignments was to get Steve Forbes on the ballot in New York. It was a very laborious, truncated process with a lot of moving parts that needed to happen in no time at all. I had to submit petitions with a total of roughly 35,000 signatures to the state of New York in order for Forbes's name to appear on the primary ballot. This is a big part of campaigning that you rarely see covered in the press. No one can vote for your candidate if he's not on the ballot. In some states, it's as simple as writing a check to the secretary of state; in other states—machine-run states—they don't want anyone on the ballot who wasn't handpicked by the Party establishment. New York was one of the latter.

The first trick the New York fixers hit you with is that they only give you three weeks to gather your 35,000 signatures. The second trick is that the machine is bound to challenge every one of your 35,000, so the general rule is that you want to collect at least twice that number. That meant I had to gather the ungodly amount of over 70,000 petition signatures to get Forbes on the ballot. As for the

Party's own candidates, they get endorsed by the Party at a state convention, which guarantees them a top spot on the ballot. They still have to get their petition signatures, but the Party does it for them, and it doesn't cost the candidate a cent.

There was another challenge—the New York Republicans hated Steve Forbes. For one thing, they didn't buy his conservative credentials; for another, he had gotten on the primary election ballot in New York State in 1996, thus making the state's Republican Party look less in control of its own process. They also illogically blamed Forbes's attacks on Dole in the 1996 GOP primaries for Dole's general election loss to Clinton. In the eyes of a lot of Republicans, Steve Forbes had cost them the presidency and they weren't about to forgive him. The plan I drew up to get Forbes on the New York ballot in 2000 called for a million-dollar budget. When I gave Bill Dal Col the estimate, he said, "Good. The last guy took two million and nearly screwed it up."

One line item in my budget was to hire some professional signature gatherers. It's a big business in New York. And back then it was all cash, so the skimming was tremendous.

Once my guys started gathering signatures, I needed a safe place to store the petitions and to serve as a base of operations. At about the same point in the '96 campaign, Forbes's New York headquarters had been robbed.

I rented an office in Queens right off the Queensboro Bridge. It's not enough to know how to fight dirty against the competition; you've also got to prevent them from using those unsavory tactics against you, so I added some precautions to the place. First I installed a security camera at the front door so you couldn't get through without being identified and buzzed in, and I hired security guards to man that door 24/7. Next I had a triple lock and a camera put on the door to the room where the petitions would be housed and bought fireproof filing cabinets to keep them in. Then I fireproofed the room itself by covering the walls and ceiling with fire blankets.

Our petitions were worth a million bucks, and it wasn't unheard of in New York political lore for a candidate's petitions to be destroyed by any manner of "natural" disaster.

We had people all over the state going door to door collecting signatures. No matter where they were or what they were doing, the moment they filled a page with signatures it had to go immediately into a FedEx envelope and back to our office in Queens.

The atmosphere was ripe for paranoia. I started looking for spies everywhere. One way was to check the phone records when the bill arrived. One time I was up in New Hampshire looking through the Queens office's outgoing calls and discovered that the campaign had been charged for a thousand dollars' worth of calls to 900-number sex lines.

I flipped out. A guy named Daryl Fox, who had worked for Giuliani, was supposed to be watching over the New York office, so I called him up and said, "What the fuck are you doing over there?" The more genteel New Hampshire campaign staffers went rigid as "Fuck!" "Fucking idiot!" and "Fucknut!" echoed from my back office—from then on I was given a wide, uncomfortable berth at the New Hampshire headquarters. I gave Daryl the times when the sex calls had been made and told him to find out who'd been on the phone then. He tracked it back to some nut he'd hired to sit in the office going over petitions but who had elected to spend all day having phone sex instead. Daryl fired the guy and I took the thousand bucks out of Daryl's paycheck.

With Forbes on the New York ballot and our petitions secure, the next thing to do was go through George W. Bush's petitions looking for suspect signatures we could challenge. The first line of defense in any election is to try to get the other guy thrown off the ballot—if you don't have an opponent, you win.

Sure enough, Dubya's team had heaped their petitions with phony signatures. One guy had filled his pages with the names of cartoon characters such as Bugs Bunny and Daffy Duck and gave all of them addresses around New York. The Party apparatus, made up of patronage hires, was getting lazy in the modern age and they were just sitting at their kitchen tables making shit up.

I called Dal Col and told him we had Bush dead to rights in at least six congressional districts. This meant that if we challenged Bush's petitions and went before a court, Bush would get tossed from the ballot in as many as six districts. Dal Col liked the sound of that. It wasn't long before he was on television in mid-January 2000 making fun of the fact that the Bush campaign had managed to locate Donald Duck and get him to sign a petition in Brooklyn.

For me, personally, this was a nice shot at the New York Republican Party bosses in Albany. They had every advantage yet still couldn't stop themselves from scheming the system.

And then reality set in. Forbes decided not to challenge. It was the first time I began to wonder whether he had what it takes to be president of the United States of America.

With the New York primary way down the road, Forbes was concentrating on the earlier ones, since a poor showing in the early state primaries would eliminate him from the later ones. We set up a press conference at a private home in Manchester, New Hampshire. Forbes was supposed to take the campaign bus from Manchester Airport to the house, then go inside and talk to the family. After a little while he would come outside and the mother and father would tell the press, "We're going to vote for Steve Forbes."

I had recently done the same thing in Delaware, with a beautiful middle-class family on a beautiful middle-class street coming out for Forbes in front of a gang of TV and newspaper reporters—a "gang" by Delaware standards is five reporters with pads, one with a tape recorder, and another with a camera. Forbes needed to do this as often as possible to show that he had traction with primary voters and shouldn't be written off as a one-issue goofball of a candidate.

I was riding to the airport to pick Forbes up in the campaign bus and everything was going smoothly. He was the only candidate in New Hampshire that day, so every press outlet would be covering him. That's when Graham Shafer, the Forbes campaign's New Hampshire director who had also worked for both Tobin and me at the RNC, called me from the press conference house to tell me that a construction crew had just arrived out of nowhere.

To this day I don't know if it was a plot or just dumb luck, but there was only one street in or out of that neighborhood and the crew began tearing it up with jackhammers.

The back-and-forth between the foreman, Graham, and me went on for so long that by the time Forbes was on the campaign bus and we were thirty minutes from the location, the crew had cut a trench across the entire width of the street that the bus wouldn't be able to cross or go around when it arrived. The clock was ticking.

The reporters and camera crews had shown up when the trench was still small enough to drive around, and now they were trapped at the house and asking Graham how they were going to get their footage of Forbes arriving in his bus.

Graham got me on the phone again and asked me what to do.

"Do? Get them to fill in the hole!" It seemed pretty obvious to me.

All Graham could muster was "Um. Okay." Clearly I didn't appreciate the dimensions of the problem.

Graham called back a few minutes later to tell me the foreman of the crew didn't seem to care that Steve Forbes was on his way.

"I'll give them five hundred dollars when I get there," I said. "A thousand, anything—just go bribe the guy! We're twenty minutes away!"

Graham went back to the crew and made his offer. "Guys, I've got a case of beer for every one of you if you can fill this hole up in the next fifteen minutes."

I stayed on the phone with Graham for the rest of the ride. At one point, he told me that a guy in a mini bulldozer was doing wheelies he was working so fast. Literally as the Forbes bus turned the corner, the crew finished filling the ditch and the press crowd burst into applause. Forbes and Dal Col were oblivious to the situation—they probably thought the cheers were for Forbes.

The rest of the event seemed to be coming off perfectly. The cameras got the shots of Forbes getting off the bus and being greeted at the door by the happy family. In the house, they had a nice little conversation about taxes and welfare reform. When they came outside, they posed for a few more pictures and a reporter asked the dad if he was voting for Steve Forbes.

"I don't know yet," he said. "I'm still undecided."

Still? It was a fucking disaster. Graham and I slunk off somewhere and got drunk.

For all his good ideas, getting the average voter to invest emotionally in someone as awkward as Steve Forbes was always guaranteed to throw you for a loop. But I knew that R. J. Johnson, the media consultant from the Wisconsin Senate race in 1998, could probably do the job. It helped that Curt Anderson knew him, too, since R.J. had briefly been an RNC colleague. In fact it was his departure that got me and the other regional political directors at the time our $10,000 pay bump. At my suggestion Curt brought him and his partner, Bill Eisner, into the campaign and they became Forbes's media consultants.

They produced a TV spot that I thought was very powerful. It showed Forbes sitting on the steps of his porch watching his family out in the front yard. To my eyes, it demonstrated Steve Forbes as the everyman, the guy with five daughters thinking about securing a brighter future for his sizable family. At the end of the ad, Forbes bows his head a bit in deep contemplation.

When we ran the spot by a focus group in New Hampshire, all the women hated it. One of them said, "When he dips his head like that at the end, it looks like he's saying, 'I have all these daughters. I hate my life! I have to get away from this family.' "

It was sad that we never could pull off showing him as a committed family man, because that's really what he was.

When I arranged a door-to-door program in Delaware for Forbes I brought Elizabeth and our son Sam, who was almost two years old. Steve's wife, Sabina Forbes, arrived in a wood-paneled Buick Roadmaster Estate Wagon with her youngest daughter, Elizabeth, who must have been around twelve years old. Elizabeth immediately took to Sam, pushing his stroller as we went from house to house.

When the volunteers and staff organized at the Delaware headquarters, I left Sam at the river that ran behind the property with a young female staffer whom I barely knew. My wife launched into me for being irresponsible when she found out where Sam was.

At the time, I didn't see what the big fuss was, so Sabina chimed in with "Of course she's angry! She carried that child in her for nine months and you let him wander off to the river with a virtual stranger? What are you waiting for? Go and get him!"

Later, when the event was over and we were driving home, Liz turned to me and said, "I don't know about Steve Forbes as president, but I like Sabina Forbes as First Lady."

— — —

In August 1999, Forbes blew a fortune establishing his presence in Iowa at the Ames straw poll—a GOP event held months in advance of the presidential primary contest when there's not an incumbent Republican. His money got him a huge tent with French doors that everyone just made fun of. French doors in *Iowa*? It was such a natural fit it stood out like pinkeye.

To deliver a celebratory atmosphere for Forbes's speech from the floor of the Ames Convention Center, the campaign's advance team arranged for a mass of balloons to float down from the rafters after he had finished his remarks, but they dropped before he even started speaking. The convention floor was full of Bushies, who of course began to stomp on the balloons while Forbes was trying to talk. No one could hear a thing coming out of his mouth. With Forbes's talent for oratory, it was just as well.

I remember thinking how perfectly it summed up his campaign—he spent lots of money on balloons and they dropped at the wrong time.

By September, Curt Anderson confided to me what I already knew: Forbes didn't stand a chance. Moreover, we knew it was Forbes's fault. When we got a look at the budget, we saw that he didn't intend to spend anywhere near the kind of money on direct mail and TV ads needed to establish a viable voter contact program in New Hampshire, but that he was going to continue throwing it away in Iowa.

The logic was that Forbes would do well in the New Hampshire primary because the state was still enthusiastic about his 1996 flat tax message and because he was the only viable conservative in the GOP primary in 2000. So now he had to win other states. Iowa was the place where they were really going to throw down with Bush. But they were picking the wrong state. George W. Bush isn't just George W. Bush—he's also his father and his grandfather. They were a political legacy and with that legacy came an organization. George H. W. Bush had been vice president and president for twelve years and he'd run twice in Iowa. There was no way Forbes could overcome that.

New Hampshire, meanwhile, was more of an open territory. There was some legacy there, but it wasn't nearly as organizationally intensive. If Forbes would spend money there, he could easily establish his own network and put boots on the ground. Instead he was going to rely on a waste of time and funds in Iowa and whatever vestiges of warmth New Hampshire still held for him from back in '96—when he had papered the state with his money.

One of the few times Forbes did squeeze out a little cash in New Hampshire for the 2000 race, it turned into the kind of FUBAR mess that would eventually become the campaign's chief identifying feature. One of the automated calls that went out to New Hampshire households was a recording of Steve saying he just wanted to call and tell the voter about his flat tax plan. Brilliantly, these calls were left on answering machines. After they went out, campaign headquarters received a flood of return calls from excited voters saying, "Hi, I'm returning Steve's call! I *just* missed him! Is he there?" This would get an eye roll, a snicker, and an answer of "Sorry, you did just miss him, but I can tell you he's counting on your support. Thanks for calling!"

"It's over," Curt told me. "Anyone who doesn't see that doesn't know what they're doing."

Sadly, campaigns are often run by people who don't know what they're doing. And knowing it was over wasn't a valid excuse for abandoning a primary candidate before any of the primaries had even gone down. As long as Forbes & Company insisted on going through the paces, all I could do was soldier on alongside them and do anything I could think of to reverse Forbes's political fortunes.

I did end up thinking of a lot of things. But I have never met a candidate so averse to winning an election.

— — —

In the weeks leading up to the Iowa caucus of January 1996, the Dole campaign had orchestrated a series of prerecorded calls to the households of Republican caucus-goers.

The message the calls delivered was along the lines of "Did you know that Forbes likes to float in balloons and ride around on motorcycles wearing leather chaps?" The "Forbes" who was a balloonist and motorcycle enthusiast was Malcolm Forbes, Steve's father. But the first thing that leaped to mind for any ultraconservative Christian Republican who received the call was "Steve Forbes is a wealthy, elite East Coast leather-boy homosexual deviant!"

I had been at the RNC in '96, and had heard about the prerecorded push-poll calls in Iowa—calls designed to lead the voters to a foregone conclusion, as in, "Would you be more or less likely to vote for Candidate A if you knew that he was a convicted felon?" Ironically, by all accounts the attack was designed and executed on Bob Dole's behalf by a gay Republican political operative. This same operative, Tom Synhorst, was now closely involved in Governor Bush's presidential campaign: his business partner, my former RNC colleague Tony Feather, was W.'s political director. And ruling them both was Karl Rove, George W. Bush's chief political strategist and the man who became a key advisor in the Bush 43 White House. By early 2000, the Forbes camp was girding for the triumvirate of Rove, Synhorst, and Feather to pull off a repeat of the anonymous leather-daddy calls. The question, obviously, was how to address it so that the attack got deflected and turned against the accuser. You certainly don't have a press conference and say "Steve Forbes does not wear leather chaps," but you can't just sit there and hope it will dissipate, because the nature of negative press is that it grows, it doesn't wither. The only thing you really can do is go on your own offensive against your opponent, and ratchet it up a notch. And surely a drunken driving charge is pretty good ammunition. The only way to stop a candidate like George W. Bush was to get aggressive—get ugly. With a network like the one that had been set up for W. as some kind of deranged birthright, there would be no chance of defeating him once he caught momentum.

But every time I or anyone else tried to suggest an aggressive message in the direct mail and on the phones, the response was always "No, we can't do that. That's too harsh."

It was shocking to me that Forbes never got indignant over the personal attacks in 1996, that he just stood there and endured it when people were talking shit about his father. At the very least you'd expect a response along the lines of "Stop talking about my family!" While most people would have wanted to shove Dole's hacks down a flight of stairs for bad-mouthing their family, Forbes wouldn't even tell them to shut their mouths. He was so emotionally tepid that people on his campaign, in 1996 and 2000 alike, seemed to be more protective of him than he was of himself. Steve Forbes should have felt the attack was unacceptable and responded in kind. But he never responded at all.

Team Bush was savaging Forbes from all sides. Rove was directing high-net-worth Bush donors to give money to Alan Keyes and Gary Bauer, two hopeless faith-based candidates, in order to drain support and attention from Forbes in Iowa. The Supreme Court says that donating money is free speech, but what are you saying when you direct money to one of your opponents in order to hurt another? If you artificially pump money into a campaign, you're giving it a bigger voice than it would have had in the natural course of the election. And it's fair that they should have no voice because the fact that they can't raise money through their own message means that their message has no value to the voters.

Then again, shame on us Forbes campaigners for failing to come up with a straw man of our own to weaken Bush.

That particular version of the Karl Rove Two-Step was extremely effective. Suddenly in certain pockets of Iowa, Bauer and Keyes were rising in the polls while Forbes was sinking.

When the polls closed at the Iowa caucus on January 25, Bush beat Forbes by 10 percent and Forbes's people actually celebrated. Throwing a party for second place was something that would not occur to most politicians, but Forbes and his supporters thought the close call indicated good things in next month's New Hampshire primary. No one mentioned that the Iowa caucus hardly counted since John McCain—Bush's true rival—hadn't bothered to run in it.

To Karl Rove, Forbes was a distraction from the real fight against McCain in New Hampshire, but a distraction is exactly that, distracting. Karl and his crew were going to make sure that Forbes didn't survive the winter in New England.

— — —

An opposition research guy who had been with the Forbes campaign in '96 went on to work for Bush in 2000. He was sure to have taken all the material he had developed for Forbes and delivered it right to Rove. At one point, Forbes went on *Meet the Press* and Tim Russert confronted him with a press release on Forbes's own campaign letterhead that contradicted his current pro-life position on abortion.

The only problem was, no such press release had ever existed. It seemed obvious to a lot of us in the Forbes camp that the Rove-managed campaign could have taken a piece of stationery that the former Forbes opposition researcher had put in its lap and produced an entirely counterfeit press release.

On the one hand, I didn't see anything wrong with it because Forbes's whole pro-life stance was as phony as Rove's fictional press release. I knew this because I was there in 1994 when Forbes campaigned for Ellen Harley in the 1994 Republican congressional primary, and Harley was the hardest of hard-core pro-choice candidates. On the other hand, the Bush team may have manufactured a piece of evidence out of thin air.

Now the test for Forbes was whether or not he had the balls to refute it. Here was his chance to stand up and call out Bush and his handlers as the two-bit lying punks that they were. Instead Forbes's reaction was to accept that the statement was true and then try to ignore it altogether.

The next ignominy Forbes would quietly suffer was at the debate in Manchester, New Hampshire. This is the big New Hampshire primary event, usually covered by WMUR, Channel 9 (aka "The House Steve Forbes Built" because of all the advertising dollars he unloaded on it in '96), the Manchester *Union Leader,* and one of the national cable news outlets. I was watching the debate in the back of the bus with Jim Tobin; Graham Shafer; Greg Mueller, who had been Pat Buchanan's press secretary in '96 and now ran his own conservative PR shop; and Juleanna Glover Weiss, who worked in the Forbes communication shop but reported to Dal Col.

This was back when reporters still had the nerve to question Bush about some aspects of his past—notably his "service" in the National Guard. But some of us on the Forbes campaign were pushing to make use of some of Bush's other weaknesses: the cocaine rumors, the drunken driving bust, and the fact that his life as a bumbling drunkard wasn't anything like ancient history.

To the alcoholism charges, Bush always responded by saying,

"When I was young and irresponsible, I was young and irresponsible," and the press had started accepting that as an answer. I found it personally infuriating. In the first place, on what planet is the age of forty a part of one's youth? In the second place, it should count. What basis do you have to judge a candidate on if not his own deeds? His *words*?

The issue had been gaining traction but it wasn't pulling Bush down. There was just a seed of him being defined as the scion of wealth and privilege saying "You know my name, you know my Daddy–It's my turn to be president."

But Forbes let Rove and the boys sucker him out of exploiting that sentiment.

The line of attack on Forbes that the Bush campaign selected was brilliant. With regimented repetition, the Bush spokespeople drummed the refrain that Steve Forbes should abstain from negative attacks–and Forbes fell for it. To Forbes's mind, he couldn't condemn Bush with rhetoric about hereditary rights because he had ascended to his own throne atop the Forbes publishing empire through his father. But it was a phony paradigm. For one thing, the idea of inheriting a family business is an American tradition older than the Constitution itself; the idea of inheriting the presidency would have made the Founding Fathers shit themselves. Moreover, Steve Forbes had been a wild success in his business; Bush the Younger had failed at absolutely everything.

That Forbes accepted Bush's rules without a sound was defining. Now Bush didn't need leather chaps or motorcycles; he had a message box that trapped Forbes.

Meanwhile, Bush's people had dug up some editorials Forbes had written in his twenties calling for Social Security reform. So the attack was "Thirty years ago Steve Forbes called for the dissolution of Social Security." This was a problem. Old people like their Social Security. If Bush's team could convince senior voters that they were choosing between Steve Forbes and their monthly check, Forbes would be gone with yesterday's trash.

Back on the bus where we were watching the debate on TV, when Bush brought up the op-ed pieces, I said, "Yeah, 'When I was young and irresponsible . . . ' It's one thing to be young and irresponsible and pen an editorial about Social Security; it's another thing to be young and irresponsible and drive drunk."

Juleanna started jumping up and down, saying, "That's the line we should use!"

She got on the phone and called up Dal Col in the greenroom at the debate site to suggest it. After the debate, Dal Col passed the suggestion on to Forbes. The reaction? Again: "No, we can't do that. That's too harsh."

That was when I knew that Steve Forbes didn't have the gumption or the guts to be the president of the United States, and that he didn't deserve to be. I remember thinking, You will never win, nor should you, because you don't have what it takes to go rip the guy's face off. Forget the frustration that he wouldn't even consider using drunken driving allegations or Bush's tortured, circumventing manner of answering questions about illegal drug use. Forbes wouldn't even refute the idea that Bush's nomination was a foregone conclusion and that he was therefore above reproach. The man wouldn't lift a finger to get himself considered a top tier candidate.

The campaign was nothing but a fool's errand. It was literally full of fools—and I was starting to feel like one myself just for being a part of the whole charade.

A week ahead of primary day in New Hampshire, I was at the storefront office in Manchester, working frantically to stave off complete campaign annihilation. Of course there was no staving it off, so I was really just trying to keep busy. I got a call from a guy named Deroy Murdock, a black conservative columnist, whom I'd never heard of at the time.

"I just wrote an article about Steve Forbes," he told me. "I'm gonna send it to you. You've got to get it out to every Republican voter in New Hampshire."

If there's one thing I know, it's that campaigns attract the freaks. I'm talking about the guy living in his car with the back window papered over with NRA pamphlets, or the freaky bag lady who comes by for coffee and donuts every day. So, as far as I knew, we had another live one here.

When I tried to put him off, he said that Joel Rosenberg, an issue research guy on the campaign, had told him to call. Rosenberg seemed like a nice enough guy, but he was outside of my chain of command, so I didn't give a rat's ass about him.

"You don't understand," Murdock told me. "You've got to do this. You need to get this article out in a piece of mail."

"I'm sorry, but that's not gonna happen."

"What are you talking about? I was told to do this."

"I appreciate that but I'm just not interested and, really, I've got to go."

"Well, you're going to hear about this."

Within a few minutes, Joel Rosenberg was on the phone yelling in my ear. "I had Deroy Murdock call and you hung up on him!"

"I didn't hang up on him, I just told him I wasn't interested."

"Well, I'm telling you, you have to do this!"

This was the wrong thing to say; now it was not going to happen, on principle.

"Well, I'm telling you," I told him, "I'm not gonna do it."

"I'm telling you! I'm ordering you!"

Finally, I said, "Look, I barely even know who you are. All I know is, you're not my boss, you don't sign my paycheck, and I'm not doing it."

"What's wrong with you?" he said. "It's game time!"

"Game time?! It's game over!" I guess he didn't get the memo.

"I'm taking this straight to Dal Col."

"Then fucking take it to Dal Col! Take it to Dal Col right now! I don't care, I've got things to do!"

The next day Dal Col called me laughing. "I got a very angry phone call from Joel Rosenberg. I told him he just got a taste of New Jersey politics. Just keep doing what you're doing."

A week later, John McCain trounced George Bush in the New Hampshire primary. Steve Forbes hadn't even been a factor. It was as if he hadn't run.

Whatever character trait it takes to do the things you have to do to steer votes away from your opponent, Forbes didn't have it. Team Bush, on the other hand, had a surplus of the stuff.

After McCain blew Bush's doors off in New Hampshire, Rove and the gang were not going to see a repeat in the next primary in South Carolina. Their data told them who the McCain supporters were in South Carolina, and they zeroed in. Just before the primary, those supporters started getting push-polling calls that asked, "Would you be more or less likely to vote for John McCain if you knew that he fathered an illegitimate black child?" They were referring to McCain's adoptive daughter, born in Bangladesh.

McCain never responded. See if you can remember how that worked out for him.

Even after the destruction in New Hampshire, the Forbes campaign grimly hung on. Forbes had beaten Dole in the 1996 Delaware primary and Jim Tobin had dreams that Forbes could repeat in 2000. But just as in New Hampshire, neither Forbes nor Tobin nor anyone else had allocated any dollars to Delaware. Despite my earlier warning to Tobin that there was nothing happening on the ground in Delaware, nobody cared to listen. All we had there was a pretty girl in a five-hundred-square-foot campaign office stacked to the ceiling with Forbes's book *A New Birth of Freedom: A Vision for America*. But I did as I was told.

I was driving to Delaware with Graham Shafer when Tobin called me up and started yelling at me about how there was no campaign infrastructure in Delaware and declared it my fault.

I yelled back, "You get what you pay for!" and we hung up on each other.

"Oh, my God," Graham said, "that felt like my parents arguing."

Forbes finally withdrew after Delaware and Tobin went to work for Bush.

Working for Bush was not an option for me, though I'm sure the transition could have been managed. Even if I hadn't known a hundred spoiled little George Bushes in prep school, I still feel I'd have developed the instinctive revulsion he inspired in me then, and does now. Our families may once have run in the same privileged, East Coast WASP power circles, but that was where the similarities ended. Perhaps it's his whole "born on third base and thinks he hit a triple" sense of entitlement, but I didn't like the guy from the minute I had laid eyes on him back in '96.

On election night 2000, I was at the Capital Hilton in Washington, D.C., where the RNC was holding the evening's election-return festivities, mostly keeping myself in the cochairman's suite. Pat Harrison was hosting, and every other head was adorned with a white cowboy hat with a sheriff's star that read "Bush/Cheney." I grabbed one of them for my son; he had the good fortune of not knowing who Bush and Cheney were, so he could really enjoy the hat. Karl Saliba and I were watching the networks in a bedroom Pat had sealed off for herself when Florida was called for Gore. I remember thinking to myself, Thank God! Bush is going to lose and I can go home.

I hung around for another few hours, breathing secret sighs of relief that the Bushies would not be moving in to the Oval Office—until the networks reversed and called Florida for Bush. Most of the country may have spent the next few weeks wondering about the results, but I knew it then and there: Bush had won. No one was taking that candy from that baby. And making a living in Washington, D.C., as a Republican had just become extremely complicated for me.

I was getting a little tired of working for other people anyway. Throughout my career I had made a good many wealthy and influential contacts. If only I could think of a solid business plan, it would be a cinch to drum up some venture capital, but what was my area of expertise?

Well, let's see . . . I did know a little something about political telemarketing.

*I*t was the year 2000, the heady height of the dot-com bubble when everyone still believed Web surfers would be willing to get out their credit cards for content other than Brazilian horse porn. A political Web site called Voter.com had just raised $50 million in venture capital; no one knew what it was, no one could figure out what to do with it, but it was on the *Internet*—how could they lose? If all it took to get venture capital for a political dot-com was a shitty idea, hell, I could easily exceed the standard.

The first one I had was to develop an online currency exchange where the Republican national campaign committees, such as the RNC, and its affiliated state parties, could log in and trade hard money for soft and vice versa. When I ran the idea by Curt Anderson, he said, "What are you, fucking crazy? This is the stuff that's supposed to happen in the dark of night."

"Why shouldn't it be transparent?" I reasoned. "It all gets filed in FEC reports anyway."

"Allen, no one's going to buy it." He was right. The currency exchange that happened almost daily between the national Republican organizations and the state parties was the equivalent of Scarface turning drug cash into Treasury bonds. No one would want to be on record doing it.

Okay, I thought, that was a bad idea; but I've got more.

My experience had taught me that the closer you get to Election Day, the fewer telemarketing vendors are available to make those crucial last-ditch campaign calls. There are only so many call centers in the United States staffed by accent-neutral Americans, and toward the end of an election they can never meet the demand of all the campaigns desperate for service because everyone's buying up that finite capacity.

My concept was to take all of the call center capacity available at any given time and publish it on a Web site. That way, instead of frantically calling telemarketers all over the country, a campaign manager could simply log on to my site and see at a glance what capacity each vendor had available. What's more, if a campaign manager needed, say, fifty thousand calls made, he could type the figure in and all the available vendors for that given day would pop up.

I would draw my Republican friends to the site, mark up the cost of the calls to a reasonable profit, and I'd take a piece off the top as the broker. All aboveboard, legal, and morally sound. Having nothing to do with the actual campaigning, it would be the cleanest job I'd ever had.

In fact, my concept would go a long way toward tidying up the elections. Up until then, candidates were routinely getting ripped off by just about everyone involved in the telemarketing process. Most campaign managers just weren't sophisticated when it came to finding vendors and understanding what the phone calls actually cost. They'd ask a pollster or a media consultant's advice and get "Oh, yeah—just call my buddy so and so." They'd end up paying six times what it was worth, and the consultant who referred them to the vendor might even get kicked back a few cents from every call.

And there were enormous fortunes trading hands, because as Election Day drew closer and closer, there were fewer and fewer places to spend campaign money. You can't develop a direct mail piece and drop it a week before the election because it will get to the voters too late, and by the final days of an election all the air time available for TV spots has been sold out. As far as paid media is concerned, the phones are a candidate's last resort.

You can place a call order up to an hour before the polls close. It's that kind of Hail Mary panic that forces the vendors to over-charge earlier in the election. When a campaign manager calls a vendor at the very last minute and asks for millions of calls to be made, the vendor can only hope he'll ever get paid for them. More often than not, a losing candidate will tell them to go piss up a rope—you know, "Go ahead, just try and collect."

With my concept, all the calls would be booked and paid for in advance. The risks for both the candidates and the vendors—not to mention the culture of kickbacks—would all be removed. My cut, the orders, the payments, everything would be done up front.

Everyone would come out a winner.

Crunching the numbers, I figured I would need about $50,000 to develop the portal and the software, and another $100,000 or so for additional setup costs. I met up with Mr. Money himself, Haley Barbour, and pitched him the idea. The meeting was at his opulent lobbying office on Pennsylvania Avenue overlooking Freedom Plaza, two blocks from the White House.

"That sounds interesting," he said. "How much money are you looking for?"

"Two hundred and fifty thousand."

"Go talk to Tony Feather."

All the call money in the upcoming election would either be coming from or be controlled by the Bush campaign, and since Feather was the campaign's political director, Haley wasn't going to invest a cent with me without Tony's guarantee that he'd be sending some of that Bush money my way. Tony also owned—and owns—a telemarketing center; he also was—and is—a partner at a company called DCI Group, founded by CEO Tom Synhorst, the Republican

who choreographed the '96 "leather chaps" attack on Steve Forbes.
Now I'd be doing business with him. Hell, if I didn't get his approval
first, I wouldn't be doing any business at all. This, I thought to myself, is how the cliché "Politics makes strange bedfellows" became a
cliché.

At the time, DCI was (and it still is) a very successful grassroots
telemarketing and lobbying company that ran all the major black-
bag operations for the Republican Party. Under Bush, it has become
the White House's external political arm.

So Tony Feather was getting paid by Bush and by his own company at the same time. But giving me a cut off the top wouldn't whit-
tle down his take any, so I didn't see there being any problem. Sure,
I didn't like Bush, but that didn't mean I had anything against
Feather or Synhorst. In fact they made more sense to me than a candidate who wouldn't defend himself against their kind of tactics—
which had been my kind of tactics all along. Besides, Bush had all
the GOP money that year, and they were the guys who decided
how to spend it.

When I went to meet with Synhorst at his Washington office, I
took an RNC old-timer from the South named Tommy Hopper with
me. Tommy and I had been colleagues under Haley. I had brought
him into my would-be company because he'd known Haley for
twenty years and I promised him a cut if he could help convince
Haley to come on board. But he was the last person in the world I
should have brought to see Synhorst.

"Don't you know he's a fag?" Tommy must have said a dozen
times before the meeting. When we got to Synhorst's office and saw
that he had shaved his head, Tommy just about went into connip-
tions, kicking me under the desk.

I asked Synhorst, "Why the shaved head?" and he explained
that he'd done it in sympathy for a friend who had cancer. I told
Synhorst that was a very considerate thing to do and Tommy kicked
me again.

I made my pitch, Synhorst said he'd let Haley know what he thought of it, and the meeting was over.

As soon as we got outside, Tommy said, "I'm telling you, he has AIDS!"

"Would you lighten up with that? He does not have AIDS, he's the picture of health! And who cares what he has and what he does with it? All I care about is him giving us the green light so Haley will give us the money."

That shut him up, but just for a moment or two. For some people, even the GOP is too diverse a community. Anyone with first-hand knowledge of the upper levels of the Republican power structure knows it could give the audience at a *Rent* marathon a run for its money. So you'd think party hacks like Tommy would have gotten over it by now, but no such luck.

Tommy was a lot more comfortable when we flew down to Bush headquarters in Austin, Texas. We were waiting for Tony Feather to come out and see us when I noticed, in the middle of a wide expanse of office space cross-sectioned by dozens of cubicles, a room enclosed on all sides by glass walls. Standing alone in that soundproof chamber was Karl Rove. It was an impressive sight, that behemoth flailing his arms while barking into a headset, surrounded by a vast blinking array of laptops, desktops, telephones, and monitors (noticeably all of the computer gear was Apple rather than PC). He clearly saw himself as a field general with his all-seeing eyes on every last troop. The effect was like something out of James Bond, or the first time you glimpse Darth Vader in his life-support pod, the bald head revealed just before the helmet comes down.

We took Feather to a Tex-Mex place for lunch and gave him the spiel. He was another one of those high-powered GOP types who made you do all the talking, but that was fine because, at the end of it, he said, "I'll tell Haley I'm all for it. I can see how we could use that." He actually went on to make a commitment that the Bush campaign would use my Web site to place some of its phone calls.

It was phenomenal. Even if they only ordered a fraction of their calls through my company, it would still be making a ton of money. At thirty-three, I had just founded what was guaranteed to be a successful political enterprise.

Back in D.C., Haley handed me off to his business partner, Ed Rogers, who had worked for Bush 41 as an assistant to the president when Haley was Bush's political director. "Ed," Haley said, "make this happen. Free up a quarter of a million dollars for Allen."

Ed is a very sharp, rail-thin Alabaman. When he and Haley had left the first Bush White House to start their own lobbying firm in 1991, Bush had chided them as an example of the revolving door in Washington, D.C., that forever blurs the distinction between politicians and the lobbyists who seek their favor. I'd been told they had opted to hide out in the Caribbean for thirty days rather than taking the political heat in Washington. By 2000, their firm was making $15 million a year with a 60 percent profit and no one was chiding them for anything they did.

The instrument Ed put together to finance my new company, GOPmarketplace.com, was called HELM, LLC. It stood for Haley, Ed, Lanny, and Mathias. Lanny Griffith was a partner in Haley's lobbying company along with Ed Rogers, and had been with Haley since they started out together in Mississippi in the early 1980s. Ed Mathias was a managing partner at the Carlyle Group—a powerful private-equity investment firm in D.C. that counts among its partners and clients ex-presidents, prime ministers, and Arabian princes, and is also ground zero for liberal conspiracy theorists.

The next five months was an arduous process of actually getting the money out of these guys—drawing up operating agreements, having discussions about how the business would be run, how the funds would be distributed, and so on and so forth. Meanwhile, I was flying around the country on my own dime trying to get the business up and running by signing up vendors and finding campaigns other than Bush's that would agree to use GOP Marketplace. I may have had Tony Feather's guarantee that the Bush campaign would use my services, but it wasn't going to be his ass on the line if that never came to fruition.

By late August the $250,000 was available. By the second week of October, I had spent $115,000 and had nothing to show for it. No one was using the site. The world of politics was not yet sophisticated enough for the dot-com era; it remained local. No campaign manager was willing to do an e-commerce transaction. They still needed names and faces. Feather hadn't placed a single order. I had a two-year-old son, my wife was a stay-at-home mom, and I was $115,000 in hock to the most powerful men in Republican politics. The 2000 election was three weeks away and my career was in shambles. One night I came home and crashed on the sofa in such an exhausted, despondent coma that Elizabeth wanted to take me to the hospital. I was a fucking wreck.

My only employee was a guy named Chris Cupit, who had been a low-level staffer on the Forbes campaign and had previously tangled with Karl Rove quite a bit while working for a congressman from Texas. By mid-October, all of our office conversation revolved around where I'd disappear to if I couldn't get Haley his money back.

We had already called everyone we could think of and had got ten nowhere. Tony Feather wouldn't even return my calls. Tommy Hopper had a piece of the company and he was totally useless. It got to the point where there was nothing left to talk about except where we might be able to find jobs after the election. If Bush won, anyone who wasn't a Bushie was out. In a rare strategic misstep, I hadn't exactly kept my opinion about Dubya to myself, and I still hadn't gone to them to make my mea culpa. Bottom line: if Bush took office, I'd have to go back to campaigning in the hinterland and work my way back to D.C.

But all of a sudden, two weeks from the election, the floodgates opened up. My old New Jersey connections came through for me and we got a ton of call orders from Larry Weitzner and Tom Blakely, who owned a consulting firm called Jamestown Associates. Their client was Dick Zimmer, a former Republican congressman from the 12th District who had lost a U.S. Senate bid to Frank Lautenberg in '96 and was now staging a comeback by trying to reclaim his old House seat. Weitzner was, and always had been, Zimmer's main political consultant.

They were running against a Democratic incumbent named Rush Holt. One of the things Weitzner and Blakely had done was to get a Green Party candidate named Carl Mayer on the ballot to suck single-issue voters away from Holt.

This would be the first of many jobs I'd do with Weitzner where we would discuss how to work the phones to use our opponent's natural strengths against him. So we made a bunch of calls to households that had been identified as green-oriented Democrats with the message "Vote for Carl Mayer–the Green Party candidate."

Our next trick was even better. Blakely called me up and asked, "How do you guys find voice talent?"

"Well, I've got a whole catalog of different voices on CDs. I've got 'single Northeastern female,' I've got 'Southern belle'–what are you looking for?"

"We're targeting Democrats of Eastern European descent using a surname select and geopolitical filter."

"Oh," I said, quickly doing the polarizing-voter math in my head. "How about 'angry black man'?"

"Yeah, that sounds good. What's *his* voice sound like?"

So I cued up one particular actor's CD on my computer and put the phone to the speaker. The track I played was one in which the actor was deliberately playing up a street gang character.

After listening for a few seconds, Blakely said, "That's the guy!"

So we had the actor record a spot over the telephone saying, "I'm calling as a Democrat, asking you to vote for the Democratic nominee. We need your vote for Holt."

I'm not saying that all Eastern European whites are racists, but, no matter where or when an election is held, there is always a cultural divide that you can rely on. The message was "I'm ghetto black guy calling you, racist Ukrainian guy, and scaring the crap out of you because you probably think that if you don't vote for the Democrat I'm going to come to your house and take care of some business."

The calls were extremely highly targeted, household by household, no message ever left on an answering machine. We wanted the message heard only by people whose reaction would be "I'm not voting for Holt because he uses scary black men to call my house."

We made calls to Democratic union households supporting Zimmer, taped by actors putting on thick Spanish accents, figuring union workers were the voters who felt most threatened by immigration. The objective was to get them to throw up their hands and stay home on Election Day. We were just forcing those people to make a decision that was true to who they really were. If you want to question someone's character, look to the people who stayed home because of those calls.

Remember—they were Democrats; *they* were supposed to be the tolerant ones.

Zimmer lost the election by 481 votes and the Green Party candidate picked up 2 percent at the polls.

The $50,000 I'd spent on the Web site turned out to be a total waste because no one trusted making an order without speaking to someone on the phone. In 2000, you couldn't tell your candidate that you placed an order on the Internet—you had to tell them whom you had spoken to and when. But it didn't matter. I just installed more phone lines at the office and hired a third person to help take the orders. A week before the election, we couldn't even handle the volume of orders that were coming in.

By Election Day, we'd made $1 million in just over three weeks, thanks to a 30 percent profit margin.

When I went over to Haley's office to pay back his investment, he said, "You know, Al, I gotta be honest with you—when we wrote you that check I thought that was money I was never going to see again."

"Well, there was a point where I thought so, too. But we managed to pull it off."

"Yeah, well, a million dollars, that's something. That's a big deal. You should be very proud of what you've done."

"I appreciate that, and I'd like to keep it going," I said.

"All right, well, count us in."

When Ed Mathias heard about the success, he told Haley, "This isn't the biggest check I've ever gotten, but it's the best return."

They got a 130 percent return on their investment in less than six months. It wasn't huge money for guys like that, but it was enough to keep them in business with me. After all, I was a product of their machine. Over the previous decade these guys had taught me the insider moves, and although it seems crazy in retrospect, they had fostered the notion that we were "family." These were my guys and we were all going to make out like bandits.

TWELVE

If Tony Feather had simply reneged on his word to use GOP Marketplace and kept all the Bush business for himself and his buddies at DCI, I'd have been fine with it. After all, Bush was his candidate and had won the presidency; to the victor go the spoils. But as soon as the next elections rolled around in 2001 he started trying to finagle my own clients away from me. There were only two statewide elections being run that year, for the governorships of Virginia and New Jersey, and Feather didn't see why I should get the New Jersey business just because it was my home turf and the Republicans there didn't give a shit about Feather and his Southern cronies.

Christie Todd Whitman was vacating her second term to run W.'s Environmental Protection Agency, and the state Party had tapped former congressman Bob Franks to be the GOP gubernatorial nominee after the initial Republican Establishment pick, state senate president Donald "Donnie" DiFrancesco, had to drop out of the race due to a potent mixture of shady land deals and a looming Clintonian variety of scandal. Franks would be facing off against Democratic state senator Jim McGreevey in the general election for governor. Franks brought in his team, which included a very good

New Jersey–based campaign manager I knew named Charlie Smith, to run the campaign. Just when everything was being set in motion, Tony Feather came barging into Trenton telling Smith that if he wanted to see any money from the Republican National Committee he had to hire DCI to do the campaign's telemarketing. It wasn't an idle threat. Feather was still Bush's political director and with Bush in the White House he effectively controlled the RNC.

Feather and his people flew in and made their presentation to Charlie Smith at Newark Airport, saying emphatically, "You don't hire us, you don't get any money."

"Okay," Smith said. "Keep your money."

If you crave the sensation of having a bag of hammers thrown in your face, try showing up from out of town and bullying a New Jersey politico. Feather and his crew were politely invited to go have sex with themselves and scamper back to Washington.

I was glad that my New Jersey guys were sticking with me, but I also knew I'd made an enemy of Feather, and that meant I'd never see any business from the Bushies—which counted me out of most of the South, the Midwest, and the mountain states, as long as Dubya was in office. On the one hand—screw them, I was doing great with my East Coast connections. And yet, money's money, and Bush's goon squad controlled so *much* of it!

As sickened by the neocons as the moderate Republicans had been in the nineties, a lot of them were positively puking on their shoes now that Bush and his entourage controlled not just the Party, but the entire American government as well. Back when the Southern Strategy began its takeover of the GOP in 1993, a group of moderates actually got together and tried to consolidate some power among themselves in the form of the Republican Leadership Council, a nonprofit political advocacy group.

But when it had become clear that Bush was destined to be the Republican presidential nominee in 2000, the high-net-worth moderates, including the big donors who founded the RLC, accepted the inescapable future and signed on to raise money for Bush.

Once Bush took possession of the Oval Office, the RLC immediately began withering under the Bush administration. It was about this time that the RLC was looking for someone with a good campaign track record and strong connections among the moderates to help revitalize it.

Larry Weitzner, the New Jersey media consultant whom I'd worked with on the Dick Zimmer campaign, offered me the position of the RLC's executive director. Weitzner was in a position to do this because he was very close to the RLC's founder, Lew Eisenberg, a top GOP donor and Wall Street investment banker with his own hedge fund. It was a terrific opportunity. The RLC was a nonprofit organization dedicated to electing fiscally responsible but socially tolerant Republicans—people just like me, people who also couldn't get any play with the Bush White House at the time. The RLC's members were high-net-worth, pro-choice, in favor of paygo tax cuts, and not obsessed with other people's sex lives. Karl Rove once told Lew Eisenberg "We like your money—we just don't like your politics." In fact they liked that variety of donation so much that Bush and Rove tapped Eisenberg to be the finance chairman of Bush's RNC.

Knowing Rove felt that way about the RLC was enough to make me sign on right there. I thought they would be great people to work with, and I knew they would make ideal clients for GOP Marketplace, but I just didn't see how the hell their organization could survive a world where Bush was President and Rove was King.

The RLC's incoming chairman was Steve Distler, a Wall Streeter who lived in New Jersey. He was an astute businessman but politically he was a bit of a novice because he really saw the RLC as an opportunity to have a voice and do good things. The fact that he was getting involved for all the right reasons is the very reason he probably shouldn't have gotten involved in the first place. Distler was less interested in currying favor with the Bushies than he was in standing up and declaring, "The Republican Party needs to be fiscally responsible and socially inclusive."

But with Bush in power no one was going to give any money to an entity that was at odds with the White House when they could give it directly to the Republican National Committee or Bush's re-election campaign and score points with the president of the United States. There were very few people who would give the RLC a donation when they could give it to Rove, have their picture taken with Bush, and get credit for the donation on a national scale.

But Steve Distler was a true believer and was ready to write the checks to prove it.

— — —

When the 2002 election cycle rolled around, Charlie Smith was running the U.S. Senate campaign of Essex County Executive Jim Treffinger in New Jersey. At the time, I was trying to position both the RLC and GOP Marketplace to be critical players in that race, so I made sure to make myself available to Smith, who had sent my company a lot of business in New Jersey's 2001 gubernatorial election.

Treffinger's main competition for the GOP Senate primary was state senator Diane Allen, a pro-choice moderate from South Jersey who had Larry Weitzner working for her—another GOP Marketplace customer. The third candidate was a nonfactor, a pro-life state senator by the name of John Matheussen who didn't have a shot at winning. The race was between Treffinger and Allen, and I had close ties to both. What to do? Play both sides until it's clear who the stronger candidate is, of course.

For either campaign to ask for my help much before the June primary would be like putting a gun to my head, but I decided early on that, if either one did approach me, I would have to do whatever they asked gratis—thereby leaving behind no FEC paper trail.

I wasn't ready to step out of the shadows when Charlie Smith called me up that January to discuss how he might cause problems for Diane Allen and John Matheussen in their home counties in South Jersey. Charlie's candidate, Treffinger, was from the northern part of the state and Charlie wanted to encourage divisiveness in the southern counties between Allen and Matheussen along geopolitical lines and around the abortion issue. Somewhere in the conversation, one of us mentioned that the Super Bowl was coming up in a few weeks. Charlie had an inspiration.

"Imagine," he said, "how pissed off you'd be if you got a campaign call during the Super Bowl."

"I don't think anyone would even answer the phone."

"But what do you think of the idea?"

"You want to call people during the *Super Bowl*?"

"Yeah, yeah!"

"Well, what are you gonna say?"

"I don't know. I'm gonna go draft a script."

He came back to me with a script that began: "I'm calling from the South Jersey Republican Party"—a group that didn't exist—and then went on to compare the ferocity of Diane Allen's pro-choiceness with the obstinacy of John Matheussen's pro-lifeness.

The calls were going to be highly targeted, going to just eight thousand Republican county committee members in New Jersey's southern counties. The content of the calls was pretty much beside the point. All we wanted to accomplish was that the committee members would end up associating the names of Treffinger's opponents with interrupting the Super Bowl when they got to their conventions and voted on which candidate to endorse—whichever candidate got the endorsement in a particular convention also got the top line on the primary ballot in that county. The people who received the calls wouldn't know which candidate had placed them, and it wouldn't matter. The only thing that would matter is that they hadn't heard the name Jim Treffinger. The pro-lifers would assume the call came from Diane Allen's campaign, the pro-choice members would think it was John Matheussen—and all of them would remember that Jim Treffinger was the pro–Super Bowl candidate.

So the calls went out, the Super Bowl viewers who received them were enraged, and how did Treffinger fare in the primary? He never made it that far. In April, two months before the primary, he ran into some complications—his home, his county office, and his campaign office were all were raided by the FBI. Turns out, they'd been investigating him for just about every political crime short of treason for two years.

He withdrew from the race and I wound up working for Diane Allen. At the end of the day, she decided to stiff me for ten grand on the bill, making the excuse that I had been working for Treffinger at the same time—which was not true.

— — —

Things at the Republican Leadership Council were just as dismal. The Bushies wanted it dead and, by the summer of 2002, I knew that they would get what they wanted—when did they ever get anything else? It wasn't enough that our money was drying up as more and more moderates elected to donate to Bush for the favor it bought them, but the RNC was starting to target anyone who had anything to do with us.

At an RNC finance meeting in San Diego, I set up an event where Arnold Schwarzenegger, who was just getting ready to run for governor of California, would address a group of handpicked potential Republican Leadership Council donors, fifteen or twenty individuals worth hundreds of millions each. Schwarzenegger was going to come and help us make our pitch, talking about the importance of having a moderate voice in the Republican Party. It was a dream scenario.

The day before the event, with everything set up and in place, Schwarzenegger's guy called me and said, "I'm sorry, but we can't come. We'd love to, but we've been told that we can't."

With that, the whole thing was in the crapper. The RNC—at Karl Rove's direction, I was told—had been calling people involved with the event and telling them to shut us down. Even Lew Eisenberg, the hedge fund master of the universe who had founded the RLC and been its biggest donor, was ordered to pull out. Rove's message was simple: "These guys are competing for our money. Stay away from them."

By the time we were limping toward the 2002 election, Steve Distler was pouring so much of his own cash into the RLC that I finally told him he was throwing his money away.

– – –

It was the summer before the 2002 general election when Jim Tobin resurfaced in my life. He had left the Forbes campaign as a moderate, had worked on the Bush 2000 campaign in New England, and, somewhere along the way, he had reinvented himself as a full-fledged, Bible-thumping, fear-mongering acolyte for the Holy Connecticut Cowboy. His transformation by the power of Christ had earned him a prominent spot as a consultant for the RNC and the National Republican Senatorial Committee.

We hadn't had any business with each other in two years, and out of nowhere he was asking me if I could have the RLC write a $5,000 check for a U.S. House candidate in Maine who was a friend of his. Tobin seemed to be testing the waters and seeing what use I could be to him. The last time I had so much as spoken to Tobin was a year before, in the fall of 2001, when both Pat Harrison and Tommy Hopper had come to me separately to let me know that he'd been bad-mouthing me professionally. I had called him on it at the time, and he had denied everything. I remembered the time that he had admitted he hated me when I first became a regional political director for the RNC just because I seemed to know what I was doing. I figured that the bad-mouthing I'd heard about was more of the same—a temporary resentment that wasn't going to have any long-term effects.

Either way, giving five grand to his guy in Maine was a zero-sum situation for me. The RLC had members who already supported Tobin's candidate, so I could just have them underwrite the donation and it wouldn't end up costing the RLC any money. In the meantime, orchestrating the donation would give me a chip to play with Tobin.

"My telemarketing company's looking for more work in the election," I told him. "Can you hook us up with some?"

Sure he could. Just like that, he gave GOP Marketplace phone work for some legislative candidates up in Maine. I figured it was either my first step toward getting back into business with the RNC after being shut out for two years, or just the political equivalent of a buyback at a bar, in which case I wouldn't hear from Tobin for another two years.

On October 18, Tobin called me at RLC headquarters, saying, "I wanted to know if you'd be willing to do some work."

"Yeah, sure. What have you got?"

"Would it be possible to disrupt phone lines?"

"Well," I said, "what do you mean?"

"If I had a couple of phone numbers that I wanted to shut down on Election Day, could you do that?"

"Anything's possible," I said, giving Tobin the example that sometimes when we did automated phone calls into small towns the volume of calls going through the switch was so big that the switch couldn't handle it and ended up shutting down. When that happened, all the lines in town would go dead until the data in the telephone switch cleared and the phone service in the town came back on line, like clearing a clogged pipe.

"Is that how you would do it?" Tobin asked.

"I don't know," I said. "I would need more information, but the answer to your question of whether or not we could shut down phone lines is, yeah, anything is possible."

"Okay. You're going to get a call from a Chuck McGee. He's the executive director of the New Hampshire Republican State Committee."

That call came a week later. "I think Jim Tobin talked to you about me," McGee said.

"Oh, yeah—you're the executive director up in New Hampshire."

"Yes, Jim told me you could help me."

"Well, Jim related an idea to me," I said. "I told him anything's possible but that I would need more information."

McGee told me that he had the numbers for the Democrats' Election Day get-out-the-vote phone banks, the lines they'd be using to arrange to get voters to the polls, to remind them to vote in the first place, and to answer any questions the voters might have.

"I've got these numbers," he said, "and I just want to shut down their operation for the day. How would you do it?"

"Well, there's any number of ways." I gave him the same example I'd given Tobin, adding, "Or, you could hire a phone center to just prank-call those numbers all day long."

"Okay, then. Let's move forward. Come back to me with an idea how to do it."

"Okay," I said.

Now that the idea was an actual reality and not a rhetorical question, I had to think through the legal ramifications.

The next day, I called Chris Cupit and said, "You're never going to believe the phone call I got yesterday." I relayed the conversation to him, and we both sort of gasped at the sheer audacity of it. To me it was amazing that an agent for the Republican National Committee would call me on the phone and ask me to do it. But the fact that the call came from the RNC is the reason I didn't just dismiss the idea out of hand. The Bush White House had complete control of the RNC and there was no way someone like Tobin was going to try what he was proposing without first getting it vetted by his higher-ups. That's if Tobin, rather than one of his bosses, had even thought of the ploy himself—which seemed unlikely.

One thing I could be absolutely sure of was that it was all going through the RNC. Because I had been in Tobin's job fairly recently, although in a different region of the country, I knew that when you worked for the RNC you were only as good as the money you brought in. And you didn't get to choose your own vendors unless you controlled the money. The fact that Jim Tobin was hiring me meant two things: first, that he controlled the money; and, second, that it was an RNC program, not a New Hampshire State Republican Party program—even if the state Party had line responsibility for implementation. I also knew that when you worked for the RNC, any tactic that didn't pass the smell test would never see the light of day without—at the very least—the approval of an RNC attorney.

The first call I made after hanging up with McGee had been to a lawyer, and not just any lawyer. Ken Gross was the Republican Leadership Council's attorney and the former general counsel to the Federal Election Commission. If anyone could advise on the legality of shutting down phone lines, it was Ken Gross.

I was very vague as to who was doing what. All I said to him was "What's the legality around running a phone program that's going to jam phone lines? I mean, in other words, that the intent of the program is to prevent an opponent in an election from being able to call out or to receive calls in."

"I don't know," he said. "Let me look into it and I'll get back to you."

Over the next ten days or so, I was going back and forth with Chuck McGee about how to implement the phone program, while talking to Ken Gross to see if it was legal.

On the McGee front, I told him he'd have to use live callers because the cost for that volume of automated calls, or "robocalls," would probably bankrupt the state Party. Technologically, you couldn't do what we did with robocalls. To use robocalls, you could reach the targeted six phone numbers in New Hampshire a hundred times in a second and a hundred thousand times in an hour. Ten hours of that would have cost a hundred thousand dollars. McGee went for the live callers plan, and said to come back to him about pricing, but I really had no idea what it would cost to hire people just to dial numbers and hang up all day. I put Chris Cupit on it and had him pitch the idea to a few call centers to see what response he would get.

A couple of guys were smart enough to say right off the bat, "I'm not touching that." Not me, of course.

Finally, we found a guy with a very small operation in Idaho who said he'd do it. Chris and I came up with a price of $15,600. Chuck McGee agreed to it, and everything was set. The only thing left was to hear from the lawyer.

It wasn't until the Friday before Election Day that Ken Gross finally had an answer: "In terms of election law, there's nothing illegal about it. I also spoke to a Federal Communications Commission attorney here"—*here* being the venerable Skadden, Arps, Slate, Meagher & Flom LLP—"who said the only problem you might have is with disruption of business, but these are volunteer phone banks, not a business. So," he summed up, "while I don't necessarily recommend that you do the program, I don't see anything illegal about it."

For me that was a green light. Everything I had learned about campaigning dictated that it was all about not stepping over the bright line of the law. You could step *up* to the bright line, just not over it. Throughout my career, "It's not illegal" was always enough to march with. Here I'd been cut out of all RNC business for the two years since Bush got elected and Tony Feather was carving it all up for himself. I figured this was the Dare—the Bushies' way of making me prove my stripes to get back into the club. To my mind, I'd do this one questionable-but-legal job, and get cut back into the RNC. Why should Tony Feather and DCI have a monopoly on it?

Everything was looking good.

At eight-thirty on Election Day morning I was making breakfast for my son when I got a call from the receptionist at the professional building where GOP Marketplace's office was located.

"Umm, a gentleman named Chuck McGee has been calling frantically for you for the past half hour," the shared receptionist told me.

Well, that's weird, I thought, and gave him a call. McGee was a mess.

"Where are you?" he shouted. "I've been trying to reach you all morning!"

"What's the problem?"

"Stop the program! Stop the program! We have to stop it immediately! The chairman says it's illegal!"

"Really? Well, if you want it stopped, we'll stop it."

"How long has it been going on?"

"Since seven-thirty this morning," I assured him. "Everything is running smoothly."

"Well, shut it down immediately!"

"Will do."

So I called Chris Cupit, and told him, "Look, I don't know what's going on, but you have to stop the New Hampshire program right now."

"All right, I'm on it."

I called McGee back at about 9:05 and told him the program would be shut down by 9:15. "Look," I said, trying to calm him down, "I actually spoke to a very good election law attorney after you first called me with this idea and he said that it's not illegal, so I don't think you have anything to worry about."

"Okay. But the program is stopped?"

"Yeah."

I never spoke to him again.

I got to the office at ten to find an e-mail McGee had sent just after eight that read, "Urgent. Chairman insists that it violates federal law. Please halt all calls."

Clearly, his morning had been one of total panic, but it was Election Day and I had a lot of other business to attend to. The

Erskine Bowles campaign, which was fighting Elizabeth Dole for the U.S. Senate in North Carolina, called up with an order for half a million phone calls. With Haley Barbour as my main investor, I didn't think it wise to take an order of that magnitude from a Democrat, so I had Chris find them another vendor and said we'd take a finder's fee. (I did have a fiduciary responsibility to make a profit.)

Later that morning, a FedEx envelope arrived from New Hampshire containing a check for $15,600.

Putting in a call to Jim Tobin, I asked him, "What's going on in New Hampshire? That guy Chuck McGee is freaking out."

"Well, I can't really talk right now," he said, "but apparently the chairman says it's illegal and doesn't want it to go forward."

The next day I called Tobin to get his take on what had happened in the elections nationally, and to feel out whether having taken the Dare was going to turn into further business for my company. It was an historic year for the Party because they had actually picked up seats in Congress in an off-year election under a Republican president.

Oh, and Republican John E. Sununu was the new United States senator from New Hampshire, having defeated Democrat Jeanne Shaheen.

In the course of the conversation, Tobin casually mentioned, "You know, the check that Chuck McGee sent you was forged."

"Really?" I said, thinking to myself, Why tell me that?

At first I wondered if I'd committed a crime by depositing the check, but then I pulled up a copy of it and saw that the last name on the signature was "Dowd," as in New Hampshire Republican State Committee chair John Dowd. It was common practice for a chairman to have an executive director like Chuck McGee sign checks for them, so I just shrugged the whole thing off and tallied up the rest of the Election Day receipts.

At end of the day, we had made $1.2 million. Despite the fact that Bush ran the Party, GOP Marketplace had made 20 percent more money than in our first year, with a steady 30 percent profit margin. All in all, it was a very good year.

Until about a month later, when I got a phone call from Lieutenant Roach of the Manchester, New Hampshire, Police Department.

"Are you Allen Raymond?"

"Yes, I'm Allen Raymond."

"Did you do some calls in New Hampshire for the Republican Party this past election?"

"Well, I'm not usually in the habit of disclosing my clients."

"That may be, but it's my understanding that you-all made some phone calls on Election Day that were highly questionable—that you guys jammed the phone lines for the Democratic Party and the Fire Fighters union in Manchester, New Hampshire."

I hadn't known it at the time, but one of the phone banks that we jammed had been run by volunteer firefighters.

"Well, I didn't know about that," I said, but I copped to the rest of it, figuring that I'd talked to an attorney and had nothing to worry about.

"I can't find anything illegal about it," Lieutenant Roach said, "but I'm telling you, you better not do anything like that again. You've now been warned."

"All right, Lieutenant Roach," I said. "I appreciate the phone call, and I won't ever do anything like that again."

I was thinking, Fuck you, you fucking hayseed—who the hell are you? If you can charge me, charge me. You're not my father, you dumbass hick.

But at the same time I was anxious. I'd been in the business of politics for a decade and had never been contacted by any law enforcement agency about anything I'd done. The way I looked at it, I was an ethical guy running a clean business. We may do some morally questionable things, but nothing illegal.

A little shaken up, I called Tobin and told him, "I just got a phone call from a Lieutenant Roach of the Manchester Police Department about the phone program in New Hampshire."

All Tobin said to me is, "What are you talking about?"

"You know—the phone program I did for you and the New Hampshire State Party on Election Day."

"What are you talking about? I have no idea what you're talking about."

"You know—the *phone jamming* program I did. The one you referred Chuck McGee to me about."

"I have no idea what you're talking about."

"Jim," I said. "Don't bullshit now. You know exactly what I'm talking about. It's the phone jamming program we did on Election Day and you know what I'm talking about."

"Oh, yeah, right," he said. "I remember."

"Well, I just got a call from the Manchester Police Department about it."

He literally said, "Okay—see ya!" before hanging up in my ear.

And I never spoke to him again, either.

I was beginning to sense a trend.

I decided not to call Ken Gross, as I thought I knew what he'd say. Later, he would deny ever talking to me about the scheme.

Over dinner, my wife said it didn't surprise her at all. "Jim Tobin is a chronic liar. That guy lies about everything. Your problem with Jim Tobin is that you intimidate him."

"What do you mean?"

She reminded me about the time he confessed "I hated you" when I'd been at the RNC for a month and appeared too organized, and how he'd ignored my warning to set up a network for the Forbes campaign in Delaware, and had then told Forbes it was my fault when nothing happened for him there. Not to mention that he had trash-talked about me to Pat Harrison and Tommy Hopper in 2001.

But I had ignored all of that at the prospect of getting RNC dollars and more campaign wins.

That was me—always the sharp-eyed operative.

— — —

A month after the Manchester police call, the U.S. attorney's office in Newark, New Jersey, gave me a ring, saying they wanted to talk to me about Jim Treffinger's GOP Senate primary campaign. I had heard that Treffinger had been arrested and indicted on something like twenty federal counts in November, but I hadn't paid much attention, not seeing what any of that had to do with me. So I went online and read the indictment.

The guy had the whole New Jersey Corruption Sampler: obstructing an FBI probe, taking kickbacks from a sewer-repair company, no-show county jobs for his friends, mail fraud—the thing read like Tony Soprano's to-do list. Ultimately, it was the twentieth count that ruined my day:

"James W. Treffinger did knowingly and willfully conspire with the Campaign Staffer and others to fraudulently misrepresent himself and a committee and organization acting under his control as speaking and otherwise acting for and on behalf of Candidate No. 1 on a matter which was damaging to Candidate No. 1. Defendant James W. Treffinger agreed to cause the recipients of the calls to form a negative opinion of Candidate No. 1 by timing the calls to occur during the 2002 Super Bowl game and mislead the recipients of the calls into believing that Candidate No. 1 was engaging in negative campaigning against Candidate No. 2."

But what really unnerved me was the kicker: "There was a Consultant who was in the business of assisting political candidates by placing high-volume political telephone messages to private residences (hereinafter, 'The Consultant')."

"The Consultant" went unnamed.

Early speculation as to the identity of the consultant landed squarely on the shoulders of the Treffinger campaign's general consultant, Dave Murray, a friend of mine who had been in New Jersey direct mail for years. But Murray had gotten the U.S. attorney in Newark, Christopher Christie, to release a statement saying he wasn't the guy. Of course, I already knew that Murray wasn't the guy—the guy was me.

I was The Consultant.

So now I had gone from never hearing a peep out of law enforcement in ten years of campaigning to getting called by two different agencies in thirty days. What the hell was going on? My stomach was a knot. As soon as I hung up with the U.S. attorney's office, I called up Pete Sheridan, a Republican Party lawyer in New Jersey whom I'd met during the Whitman campaign in '93.

"Hey, Pete, uh, I just got a call from the U.S. attorney's office up in Newark. They want to talk to me about the Treffinger race and I think I need legal counsel. Can you represent me?"

Being a Party lawyer in New Jersey, Pete had too many ties to Treffinger to get involved, so he referred me to another attorney, Bob Stevens, who signed on for a $5,000 retainer. It seemed like all I ever did was hand out $5,000 checks. Stevens scheduled me for a meeting with Assistant U.S. Attorney Nelson Thayer in Newark on February 7. This was February 1.

My next call was to Steve Distler at the RLC.

"I've just got to be very upfront with you about something that's going on," I said. Laying out the situation, I told him, "This thing just came up in New Jersey. I don't think I have anything to worry about, but you should know that the U.S. attorney's office in New Jersey is going to be questioning me about one of the counts on Jim Treffinger's indictment."

"Oh, okay. Well, just sit tight. I don't think it's a big deal."

That was easy for him to say. Internally, I was freaking out.

"Steve, I anticipate that I'm going to have to resign from the RLC."

"No, no—you're jumping the gun. Just slow down and let's see what happens."

"All right," I said. "But if the time comes, I'll resign. You don't have to fire me, okay?"

"We'll just wait and see what happens."

Despite all the half-assed reassurances, my freaking out continued unabated.

I was online checking every newspaper in New Hampshire and New Jersey by five o'clock every morning. My wife thought I was crazy. Every time she saw me anxiously clicking through article after article, she'd say, "Would you calm down? There's nothing to worry about." But something just didn't feel right. With a career like the one I'd had, I knew the subtle sounds and scents of a shitstorm brewing.

On February 7, a few hours before I'd be taking the train to my questioning in New Jersey, sure enough there was a thrilling little read on the *Union Leader*'s Web site: "Federal Officials Alerted By Police to Alleged GOP Phone-Jamming."

My thoughts? Fuck *me*!

I was destroyed. Maybe that supersleuth Lieutenant Roach couldn't find anything illegal about what I'd done, but now the feds were going to have a shot at it. I felt like a guy in a car sliding off an icy road. "Oh shit, oh shit, oh shit!" was playing through my brain on a nonstop loop.

It was a stroke of luck that there turned out to be a blizzard that day and the assistant U.S. attorney in Newark pushed back the interview a week—my mind was too much of a car crash to stand up to questioning at the moment. I stayed home reading and rereading the article like a condemned man with a Bible. Personally, I found the story fascinating. It was about all my new friends in New Hampshire.

There was the good Lieutenant Roach, requesting the federal investigation, and even old Chuck McGee, the man who hired me for the job. But according to the paper, Chuck must have been stricken with some sudden and debilitating mental disease, because he couldn't remember anything about anything.

He said he'd "vaguely" heard of GOP Marketplace but that he "did not hire the firm." Then the new chairman of the New Hampshire Republican State Committee, Jayne Millerick, said all of it had occurred "before my time" and that she "knew nothing about jamming the opposition's phone lines."

I knew immediately where I stood. This was not a political matter; it was a criminal matter. We had crossed over that bright line and they were hanging me out to dry. There was no reason for me to call anyone involved because McGee had just made the statement for everyone: Allen Raymond did it—he's the bad guy.

I was already lawyered-up in one state; now I'd make it two. I called an old college roommate of mine, who was an attorney in Virginia, and asked if he knew any good lawyers in New Hampshire.

"Yeah, I've got the perfect guy for you. His name is John Durkin. I went to law school with him at Catholic University and his dad was the Democratic U.S. senator from New Hampshire."

So I called Durkin, told him the situation, and he said to send him $15,000. I was now in the business of writing checks to lawyers, and it would be my vocation for the next three years.

The next morning, at my five o'clock wake-up, I saw that McGee had changed his story. He was now acknowledging that he had hired GOP Marketplace, but to do something entirely different than jam the phone lines. That was interesting, since I had only spoken to the guy three times in my life and we'd never talked about anything else. But he was a bighearted sort. He was resigning his position so as "not to become a distraction to the New Hampshire State Republican Party."

It was a new wrinkle to consider: they were throwing him under the bus, too.

I was pissed. Jim Tobin and his guys at the RNC were covering their asses. They couldn't have handled things more ineptly. If they were going to sacrifice Chuck McGee anyway, they should have done it, accepted responsibility, and the story would have gone away. Instead they were clearly going for the old-school cover-up, that tried-and-true political tactic that has taken so many scandals and turned them from temporary embarrassments into the stuff of impeachment and prison for some of the most powerful people of any party, in any time, anywhere.

Before I went to my appointment with the U.S. attorney at the federal courthouse in Newark, Bob Stevens had gotten an assurance that they were only interested in me as a potential witness and not looking to file any charges, but you wouldn't know it from the way those guys acted when I showed up.

There were two assistant U.S. attorneys and an FBI agent, and the feeling in the room was pure hostility. I spent the first two hours or so detailing for them my political résumé, which listed fifteen different job titles in ten years, which was hardly out of the ordinary in that particular field.

"As you can tell," I said, "this isn't a line of work that offers a lot of job stability."

"That or you got fired a lot," one of them shot back.

"How did the Super Bowl script come about?" asked another.

"I worked on it for Charlie Smith."

They asked me if I thought it had been a good idea to place calls that pretended to be one Treffinger opponent attacking another. I had to point out that the calls didn't actually pretend to come from any of the candidates, but from a fictional third group—the "South Jersey Republican Party."

Boy, did they hate that answer.

One of the guys questioned my ethics, saying, "Well, didn't you know it was wrong?"

In ten years, no one in my professional life had ever questioned my ethics. It had literally never come up.

"Well," I said, "there really is no right and wrong in politics. There's legal and illegal. It's really all about perspective. Just because you have a badge doesn't give you any better perspective than anybody else. If you want to tell me it's illegal, well, that's up to you. But as far as my ethics? My ethics are fully intact."

We had been going back and forth for about four hours when the FBI agent said, "We want to play you a recording."

They took me downstairs, where they stopped at the door to a room and the FBI guy told me, "Wait out here for a minute."

They went into the next room and I could hear them playing tapes. After listening at the door for a minute I figured out that they were tapped phone calls. Next, I heard my own voice and the sound of my feet pacing back and forth as I was talking on the phone. I had an instant moment of clarity where I could see myself in my living room in Georgetown, pacing the borders of our aqua-colored Oriental rug while I was talking about the Super Bowl calls with Charlie Smith.

It was a frightening moment. Not that I had lied to the feds or concealed the truth, but to find out that the government had been listening while I was in my own home talking on the phone was deeply unnerving. I froze up, just starting to realize the reach these men had. It was beyond intimidating. In that moment it seemed to me that the government could pick anyone off the street, throw them in prison, and you'd never see them again.

I had come to find out that that was closer to the truth than I had ever imagined.

They brought me into the room and played me the actual call that went out during the Super Bowl. At the end of it, one of the assistant U.S. attorneys said, "See what we mean? You're posing as one candidate attacking the other."

"It does sound like that," I admitted. "But you skipped the beginning where she says, 'I'm calling from the South Jersey Republican Party.' "

"That doesn't matter!"

As intimidated as I was, a little courage decided to sneak in. "That matters a lot," I said. "You guys are completely wrong. You have to look at the indictment."

I had the Treffinger indictment with me, so I turned to the first line of the twentieth count, which charged "conspiracy to fraudulently misrepresent campaign authority."

"Well, that's not what we were doing," I said. "Look, all we're doing is talking about issues. The fact is that these candidates' positions on abortion are documented. These were their positions—they can't deny it. They may not like being confronted with the truth, they may not like that we presented it during the Super Bowl, but it's true."

While I had a head of steam going, I forged on with "And while the South Jersey Republican Party may not exist, we weren't posing as one of the candidates. Polling companies do it all the time. They'll say they're an organization that doesn't exist to avoid disclosing who's conducting the survey."

The whole thing took six hours, at the end of which they told me they'd get in touch when they needed me to testify.

From the federal courthouse, I went straight to a Portuguese restaurant in Newark where Steve Distler had set up a lunch meeting for us.

After we ordered, Steve asked about the questioning. "It was fine," I said. "I'm just a witness. I'm not being charged with anything."

"Well, what do you know about New Hampshire?"

"Honestly, all I know is what I read in the papers. I've hired an attorney, but I don't know where it's going."

The waitress arrived with our orders. She brought me this beautiful, steaming platter of paella. I was emotionally drained, physically wiped out, and starving. I couldn't wait to dig in.

I had barely opened my mouth when Steve said, "Everyone feels you need to resign. I'm asking for your letter of resignation. You need to leave the RLC."

I had never been fired in my life—I had had no idea what it felt like. Apparently it obliterates your appetite. I knew right there that I was done forever in politics. My career was finished. Ten years to fashion, one week to obliterate.

"Eat up," Steve said, "eat up. It'll be fine."

"You'll have my resignation tomorrow."

"No, I'll keep you on for a month. To make the transition."

I'm still grateful for that gesture. Anyone who was more of a politician would have just stormed out and stuck me with the bill.

THIRTEEN

Once Distler told me I was out of the Republican Leadership Council, the rest of the conversation was white noise. I left my heaping plate of seafood untouched and stumbled to the train station in a daze.

Over the next couple of weeks it became clear that my questioning over the Treffinger scandal was going to seem like an annoying little dinner chat compared with what was in store for me in New Hampshire. A blog called PoliticsNJ.com broke the news that I was the unnamed informant in Treffinger's indictment, but I was barely paying attention to New Jersey anymore. The Jersey feds didn't have anything to threaten me with—New Hampshire was another story.

The papers up there were running Republican phone jamming stories every day and the New Hampshire Democratic Party was calling for the heads—and other morsels—of every Republican to whom they could possibly link the scheme. Of course, I knew that I was on my own as far as the GOP was concerned, so all I could do for the time being was watch and wait. Having over a decade of political crisis management under my belt, I understood what their objective was: "Distance ourselves from the stench." Every Republican

I knew started putting as much space as they could between themselves and me.

Just after Chuck McGee resigned, his bosses developed a new version of the Election Day merriment. Now the tale they were pitching to the papers was that I had stolen their money, that the New Hampshire Republican Party had paid for my services but that I had decided in my own roguish way to design and execute the phone jamming operation without anyone's approval—indeed, without ever telling a soul!

Admittedly, this was a thrilling tale. And they were only disregarding the puniest facts. For instance, they neglected to mention that I only received that $15,600 check *after* every man, woman, and beast in the state of New Hampshire was pretty sure that the Republicans had jammed the Democrats' phones. Or that at 8:05 A.M. on Election Day, their executive director had sent me an e-mail reading, "Urgent. Chairman insists that it violates federal law. Please halt all calls." In their half-assed rush to the press, they had skipped the due diligence of the vulnerability study.

— — —

The rest of the winter was a gray blur of anxiety. Three months after they began floating the story that I was a thief and a liar, I got a letter from James Merrill, an attorney for the New Hampshire Republican Party, demanding their $15,600 back.

Even I had to take a step back and admire the audacity. They were going to throw me under the bus, but first they wanted to check my pockets to see if there was any cash in there. The *balls* on these guys!

I sent the letter over to John Durkin, telling him, "I am never giving them their money back. There's no fucking way."

"Of course not. If you give back the money you'll be admitting to what they're saying about you. I'll pen a letter."

After some lengthy legalese about why they would never see a cent of that money again, the last line of the letter was "I trust there will be no further communication regarding this issue."

Meanwhile, the press in New Hampshire rarely let the story take a day off to relax, because when they did, the head of the New Hampshire Democratic Party, Kathy Sullivan, made them put the thing back to work again by asking all the right questions—"Who knew what?" "When did they know it?"

The Republicans had the same answer over and over again: "Allen Raymond did everything—and he did it all by himself!"

I didn't know if the FBI had heeded Lieutenant Roach's call for an investigation, but Sullivan was renewing the battle cry in every edition. She wanted someone, anyone—everyone—prosecuted, to the full extent of the law and beyond. And if there weren't any laws on the books that covered what we'd done, well, she'd just grab a batch of other laws and use *them*. For both parties, it was just more politics—with me as the sorry son of a bitch in the middle.

Kathy Sullivan tried to make the case that the U.S. Senate race had been stolen and that Senator-elect Sununu's claim to the office was tainted. Sununu had won by 19,751 votes, too many to attribute to an hour and a half of phone jamming, but a number of Democrats farther down the ballot had lost by less than two hundred votes.

With all the reporters digging around, I spent seventy-two hours straight that February trying to make as much of myself disappear from the public domain as possible. I shut down GOP Marketplace's Web site, had the Webmaster remove its cached presence from the Internet, closed the offices, and let Haley and my other investors at HELM, LLC, know that I would do whatever I could to keep them out of the whole mess. Haley was running for governor in Mississippi and he didn't need the headache. Besides, it wouldn't be fair to have him mixed up in this when all he had done was back my company.

It seems ridiculous to me now that I still gave a crap what happened to those guys, but at the time I couldn't shake the sense that I owed my mentors that much even as they were digging a hole in the desert with my name on it.

I shouldn't have worried, because it turned out that a little election scandal couldn't rattle a guy like Haley and his HELM partners. When I paid them back the $50,000 that I owed them, they turned it back to me to invest in another company I was starting that would offer the same services as GOP Marketplace with a new name and offices in Georgetown.

— — —

In May, Chris Cupit got a call from the receptionist at our old GOP Marketplace building. She told him that the FBI had been all over the place. Four agents had shown up asking questions about us. Now I knew there really was a federal investigation going on. Even though it seemed like half the GOP was libeling me at every chance they got, I thought I might be able to reach out and make them see things from my perspective—namely, that if I was going down, I wasn't going quietly, and I wasn't going alone.

I reached out to Tony Feather at DCI, an unlikely ally to be sure. We had competed over clients, and he had shut me out of the RNC business for two years (along with nearly every other Republican telemarketing vendor), but if I could make him see how my problems could affect his business, he might bring some pressure to bear in the right places. He was certainly cutthroat, but he was honest in a cutthroat's kind of way. We understood each other.

We met for breakfast at a café at Twenty-first and M streets in D.C. and I laid it out for him.

"Jim Tobin is the linchpin. He's the guy who put this whole thing together. Look, you don't need to worry about me. I'm not going to talk to the press, I'm not gonna cause any problems. I'll weather this thing and at the end of the day it'll all work out, I'm sure."

Then I got to the point of the meeting: "But if the feds ever come knocking on my door, all bets are off—I'm telling them everything. Because then it's about me and my family and our future. Then it won't be about allegiances, Party, or any of that rah-rah take-one-for-the-team bullshit. If the feds come to my door, I'll bring this right to yours. I'll bring it right to the RNC.

"That's not a threat," I assured him. "That's just the reality. And you should know that. You should know that *now*."

"Okay, fine, fair enough," he said. "I hear you. I'll have a few conversations."

To me, it was a political case that Bush's Department of Justice could quash to protect the RNC, once the RNC understood that it needed protecting. This was back when Bush's people made inconvenient truths go away all the time. None of that had caught up with them yet. I was assuming that Tobin, and his cohorts at the RNC who knew about the program, were keeping tight-lipped about their involvement down at GOP headquarters.

If the yokels in New Hampshire wanted to charge me locally, that was fine—I'd just never set foot in New Hampshire again. It was those damn feds I had to worry about.

The next person I met with was Mark Miller, the right-hand man to RLC founder Lew Eisenberg, who was now Bush's finance chair at RNC. My rationale was to put it in as many heads as possible at the RNC that their operative's key role in the New Hampshire fiasco would become the stuff of raging headlines and shock-feigning editorials if they let the Democrats make a federal case out of it. I wanted to shake things up enough that somebody at the RNC involved with Tobin's scheme would feel the tremors and break ranks.

Mark and I hooked up at Union Station. He sounded sympathetic. "You're getting screwed," he said. "This is wrong. I can't believe Tobin's involved. Who else knows?"

"I told Tony Feather and I'm telling you. Nobody else knows."

Mark pumped me for more information and I was happy to give it to him because I was desperate for friends.

"That's incredible," he said. "Well, that really sucks for you. I'm sorry to hear it, but I'll get word to Lew and make sure he knows what's going on."

If Feather or Miller ever did get word to anyone, it didn't help.

— — —

I was driving back to the Georgetown office from a luncheon one afternoon in July when it happened. Chris Cupit called me on my cell phone.

"There are two FBI agents here. They have a subpoena and they want to talk to you." I just kept driving for a minute, trying to decide whether to go to the office and confront it head-on, or whether to run from it for a little while longer. Chris said, "Why don't you just go home?"

Then I realized that if I went home, the feds would just go there, too. It was bad enough to have them where I worked; I sure as hell didn't want them invading the place where I slept with my wife and played with our kids—Elizabeth had given birth to our second son, William, a year before.

I thought, Fuck it. "Go tell them I'll be there in fifteen minutes. Tell them I'm happy to talk to them."

It was an exceptionally hot day, but I was so nervous just then that I stopped sweating. Of all the headline-grabbing crises I'd been involved with, this one was all mine. As I closed in on the office, it began to dawn on me that all those other battles hadn't really mattered. Of course they had meant the world to me at the time, but only through the narrow focus of momentary ambitions. What had the great overarching vision of my life been? A five-year plan I'd devised when I was a twenty-three-year-old grad student who'd never even been in the game.

I had gotten a lot of people elected to a lot of powerful positions—for what? What had they done for the country? What had I expected them to do? The fact was, I'd never really cared. Every time someone talked policy, to me it was just more campaign propaganda, just some more of the old blah-blah-blah. My thoughts on policy had always been, If I've listened this long, then whoever is speaking owes me a pizza; now let me get back to spinning. If they won, I gained more clout; if they lost, I found another campaign—and then I gained more clout.

Now it seemed I didn't even have clout enough to accomplish the one thing that most Americans manage to succeed at without ever even thinking about it: staying out of jail.

I parked the car feeling strangely invigorated—shaken, but not a quivering wreck. If I could manage a crisis that I had no truly personal stake in, I wasn't going to suddenly forget everything I'd ever learned and shit my pants the first time my own ass was on the line.

When I got into the office, the receptionist pointed out the agents, a man and a woman, and said, "Those two people are waiting for you."

I walked right over to them. "Hi, my name's Allen Raymond. What can I do for you?"

"Well, we'd like to talk to you."

"Sure. Come right in."

I brought them into my office, but didn't sit down, and didn't offer them a seat. There was no need for them to get too comfy when I wanted them to leave.

"Well, what can I do for you?"

"We have a subpoena."

I remembered what John Durkin had told me to do if any feds ever showed up bearing papers: "Be very pleasant, take the subpoena, and tell them verbatim, 'My attorney will contact your office to set up an appointment.'"

So that's what I told them.

"Well," the male agent said, "you know, you can talk to us right now and tell us what you want to tell us."

"I appreciate that, but I think it would be better if I work through my attorney."

The female agent explained, "Well, we really think you should talk to us now."

"I appreciate that, but I really think it would be better if I talked to you at another date, set up by my attorney."

The male agent: "Yes, but I think it would be better for you to talk to us now and tell us what you know."

In my head, the old "Who's on first?" routine was playing, and I started to wonder how long we could keep this back-and-forth banter going.

"I'm going to tell you everything I know," I assured him. "I just can't do it today. I'll do it when my attorney sets up an appointment."

They left and I collapsed in my chair, thinking, Here we go.

— — —

Before my interview with the FBI, I made a decision. This was going to be a game of musical chairs, and no fucking way would I be left standing. When the music stopped, I wanted to be seated as comfortably as possible. Jim Tobin had clearly stated his position by saying "I have no idea what you're talking about" when I'd brought up the phone jamming the last time we spoke. He was the Republican Party's boy, and he stood quietly in its gloom while it called me a liar and thief. So fuck Jim Tobin, and fuck the Republican Party.

Over a telephone call, Durkin laid out my options: fight or cooperate.

"If you go to trial," he said, "it will cost you a whole lot more money and the outcome is probably incarceration and a hefty fine. We don't know what they're charging you with yet, but we do know there were eight hundred and some-odd phone calls made. Which means, whatever they do charge you with, there could be eight hundred counts. You could be looking at twenty-five years in prison."

"Get the fuck out of here! Twenty-five years in prison?"

"I'm not saying they're going to do it. I'm just giving you the range of things that can happen to you. And if they really feel like they want to get you, they can put an extraordinary amount of pressure on you. The government can do anything to you that it wants."

While I pondered that little chestnut, Durkin asked, "What is your disposition? Is your disposition to take on the federal government, or is it to cooperate?"

"My disposition is not to go to jail."

"I can tell you this," Durkin said. "The government only brings cases that they'll win. These guys win ninety-five percent of their cases."

That 95 percent figure had a powerful resonance with me—it was the same probability an incumbent has of winning an election. I knew that it was only under the most unusual circumstances that an incumbent was defeated. And in federal court, the government was the incumbent.

I didn't have any polling data, but just taking a quick lay of the land I arrived at some conclusions: they're in control; it's their court system; I've been painted as a maniac and a villain and a thief by the very people who employed me, and whose government was more securely in power than any administration in half a century.

Still, I was hanging on to one last shred of hope.

"But I talked to an attorney before I did anything. He said it wasn't illegal."

"Do you have that opinion in writing?"

"Well, no, but I have a bill."

"A bill's not going to save you."

"Now, wait a minute," I said. "Why can't I say in court that I got an attorney's opinion?"

"Lawyers hate that kind of thing. If you can't show it in writing, don't say it unless you want to piss off the judge."

"Don't piss off the judge? Why not? That's not fair."

"What do you expect? At the end of the day, we're all lawyers. No judge is going to give up one of his own. You'd be setting a precedent that none of us want set. I give people advice over the phone all day long and I don't know *what* I'm saying half the time. If I had to worry that it was my ass every time I talked, I'd never talk to any-one."

In the end, we had no idea what they'd charge me with, but whatever it was, I'd cooperate.

— — —

When I told Elizabeth that I knew I was going to end up getting hit with a criminal case, she said, "You're crazy. How can that be?"

"Because it's going to be a witch hunt. None of it is going to be about the law; it's going to be about the law being used as a means to a political end. I'm going to get fucked in this whole thing and you need to be prepared for it."

"At the end of the day," Elizabeth said, "it comes down to who you are. When you're alone and confronted with yourself, do you like what you see?"

"I don't think what I did was so wrong, but other people may, and it's all incredibly politically charged. They're going to want someone's head and that head is gonna be mine. There're four kinds of judgment: family first, then community. After that it's law and power. Clearly I'm no longer family, Tobin's seen to that. I'm not from New Hampshire, McGee is. So that leaves me with law and power and both are against me here. They won't want to nail one of their own when they've got some faceless Republican consultant from D.C. they can do it to. Next to Al Qaeda, I'm the easiest thing to hate. They're gonna paint a picture that says I'm what's wrong with the process."

Elizabeth said, "Okay, what is it that we tell Sam and William every day? 'Tell the truth, be honest, don't be mean to people—be the kind of people who can be proud of themselves every day.' Now it's time to demonstrate all that through your actions."

When I thought about it, telling the truth would be easy. For one thing, it was the only chance I had. For another, everybody had it coming.

The last thing Elizabeth told me was "This is not the worst thing we will ever go through as a family and this is not going to destroy our family. We're stronger than that; nobody is going anywhere. I'm not going anywhere. Whatever happens, I'm going to be here, we will be here. This family will remain intact."

— — —

On September 8, the proffer from the Department of Justice (DOJ) arrived at Durkin's office for me to sign. It established that I was going to cooperate with the investigation, sit for interviews with the federal authorities, and tell them everything I knew, and that if criminal charges did arise, I'd be pleading guilty. On my side of the bargain, the government couldn't use anything I said to establish charges against me unless they could substantiate it with a third party, but they could use my testimony against me for sentencing purposes.

I signed it, throwing myself on the mercy of the court.

The one thing I wanted to add to the agreement was a guarantee that, when it came time for sentencing, the hearing wouldn't take place in New Hampshire, before a New Hampshire judge.

Durkin pointed out my dearth of options. "You want to be a rich white guy going before a judge in D.C.? There *is* no good jurisdiction."

I still decided that I needed to have a D.C. lawyer—preferably a black woman, preferably a black woman who used to work in the Department of Justice. Pamela Bethel was all of those things, and an excellent attorney. With another retainer check of $15,000, I signed her on a week before my first interview with the DOJ.

— — —

Durkin flew down from New Hampshire and we got together at Pamela's brownstone office right off K Street for the final preparation for my interview at the DOJ that day.

"Go in there and be you," Pamela advised me. "You're not what they think you are."

What the DOJ was expecting was a slimy D.C. scoundrel in a Gucci suit, French cuffs, tassel shoes, and a fat watch. I had accounted for such generalizations weeks before the interview and had taken appropriate measures. I owned three watches worth $6,000 altogether, so I went and bought a twenty-five-dollar Timex at CVS and scuffed it up for four days while I was playing with my kids in the yard to make it look like I'd been wearing it forever. I pulled out clothes I hadn't worn in ten years—a button-down shirt with frayed cuffs and collar, a power tie from 1990, and the first suit I ever bought when I got out of college. I did wear a pair of tassel loafers, but they were ancient and one of them had a hole in the sole.

In politics, presentation is everything. When I presented myself to the DOJ, I wanted them thinking, Look at this poor jerk. Man, is that pathetic. No way is this guy a mastermind of anything.

When I had put the whole ensemble together, Elizabeth just clucked her tongue and gave me the thumbs-up. And then I jumped into my Audi and went to my meeting.

Back at Pam's office, Durkin told me, "Tell them everything."

"Well, what do I tell them about me having a conversation with a former lawyer for the FEC?"

"If it comes up, I'll excuse you from the room and have a conversation with them."

Unlike so many of my clients, I decided I would listen to my advisors. Half my candidates had only been interested in whether I'd brought money to the table; the other half would listen to me until they decided I was telling them things they didn't want to hear. But I knew enough to admit when I was out of my element, and I'd never seen a criminal investigation from any closer vantage point than a TV screen. Besides, between my two attorneys, I had $30,000 on the table, so I figured there was value in what they had to say.

Just as it is for a candidate in a campaign, my main objective in this first encounter with the feds was to define who I was. As in any election, there is always what you say about yourself and what your opponent says about you. I knew what my opponents were saying. This was my first opportunity to say something for myself, to define who I was for these people who held my future in their hands. I had to come off as likable, cooperative, and humble. I had my talking points.

And as I had always told my clients, "Stick to the freaking talking points. Don't freelance."

Inside a nondescript office building at 1306 New York Avenue, a block from the White House, there was wall-to-wall uniformed DOJ security. We were processed through security, and given visitor's badges printed in ink that turns invisible after about eight hours; then I met my prosecutor.

Todd Hinnen, the DOJ trial attorney for my case, was a few years younger than me, good-looking, blond, about six feet tall, very neatly dressed, and personable. He smiled at Durkin, smiled at Pam. Then the smile disappeared as he shook my hand and said, "Good morning, Mr. Raymond."

He brought us upstairs to a conference room, where I met agent Kathy Fuller, the FBI's lead investigator on the case. She looked very intimidating—well, the holster-bulge on her hip looked very intimidating. But I was ready to rumble, in a humble sort of way. I had already been through an FBI interview, so I knew that first chunk of it was going to be all about my biography. I think they do it to loosen up their witnesses, the same way you get a person to talk about him- or herself at a cocktail party.

After an hour or so of icebreaking, we started getting down to business. As I laid out what had happened in New Hampshire, one thing was clear: this was a version of the events they had never heard before. They had never even heard the name Jim Tobin or been told about Chuck McGee's role in the affair.

I gave them all the McGee e-mails, which included the one in which he had placed his order for the calls, as well as his final frantic plea to shut down the program—not to mention the missive in which he provided me the list of phone numbers to be attacked. On the paper copy of that e-mail, I pointed out the icon that designated that an Excel spreadsheet had been attached.

"What was on the spreadsheet?" Hinnen asked.

"Usually, when we get these spreadsheets," I explained, "they've got thousands, if not tens of thousands—if not hundreds of thousands, or even millions—of phone numbers on them. This one had six."

"And what other conversations had you had with McGee?"

I told them about our second conversation. I had asked him how he came up with the idea to jam the phones. I mean, it was a very unusual idea. I'd been through a lot of campaigns and had never dreamed it up.

"Well," McGee had told me, "I used to be in the military, and one of the things they taught us was to disrupt your enemy's lines of communication. So I just applied that lesson to politics."

If they teach warfare at the Graduate School for Political Management, why not teach political management in the military? With our system, it comes to the same thing.

That conversation with McGee was an important detail to give the feds, because how else would I have known that McGee had served in the military? I mean, Bush's GOP wasn't a place where you could just assume most of the men had served in uniform—you could hardly find one who did.

When I told them that Tobin said McGee had forged the chairman's signature on my check from the New Hampshire State Republican Party, it further proved my honesty, because it turned out to be true. And how would I have known *that* if Tobin hadn't been up to his eyes in the New Hampshire program? I'd never seen the chairman's signature in my life.

I was giving them the facts as fast as they could write them down, but I was also trying to entertain them. I wanted to bring them into my world, to make them see things from my perspective so that they might be able to understand why I had done what I'd done. All along the way, I was peppering the account with humanizing details—that once a month I go out to feed the homeless with our church (a progressive church with a gay priest who preaches from the Gospels instead of Revelation, and where no one ever handles a snake), that I have two kids, and that I married my college sweetheart.

When I told them about all the madness of Election Day morning, I made sure to mention that I remembered getting that first phone call in my kitchen because I'd been making breakfast for Sam. It was true, so what kind of a moron would leave it out?

Hell yes, I was spinning for all I was worth. But for the first time, all I was worth actually depended on it. I wasn't doing it so some platitude-spewing hack could be elected Grand Cyclops. I was doing it for my freedom, which happened to have the happiness and security of my family riding on it. Who on earth wouldn't sink every damned politician in the world for that?

And here was another first: I wasn't spinning truth with lies—I was spinning truth upon truth upon truth.

Call it a deathbed conversion, but it was a conversion nonetheless.

At the end of six hours, Hinnen and Fuller's demeanor toward me had completely changed.

As Bethel, Durkin, and I were leaving the building, Pamela turned to me and said, "That was a huge success."

Durkin added, "You are no longer who they thought you were."

I was no longer the only one who'd get fucked; we had successfully conveyed that I was just the little fish that could lead the way to the big fish. And when those big fish found themselves gutted, scaled, and sizzling in the pan, they could never say I didn't warn them.

FOURTEEN

By 2004, about the only people in government who would have anything to do with me were my DOJ prosecutor and my FBI investigator. My political career was finished. In the 2003 elections, I'd done about $250,000 worth of business, down from $1.2 million the previous year. A few of my old friends from New Jersey had sent me that work. To the rest of the Party, I was a dead man.

It was just as well that I shuttered the company, because I had a new full-time gig: I was senior vice president of keeping my ass out of prison.

At one point, John Durkin related to me a conversation he had had with Todd Hinnen in which Hinnen said, "This has gone all the way to the top."

"Well, what does that mean?" I asked. "All the way to the top DOJ, or all the way to the top White House?"

"All the way to the top DOJ. This is on John Ashcroft's desk."

"Okay, so what does *that* mean?"

"I don't know what it means, other than that Ashcroft is calling the shots."

I didn't know if that was good or bad, but I thought back to my

one encounter with John Ashcroft, before Bush had tapped him
to be attorney general. He was running for reelection to the U.S.
Senate in 1999 when I was working for Mitch McConnell at the
National Republican Senatorial Committee. I'd been called to a
meeting at Ashcroft's office between Ashcroft; the RNC's political
director, David Israelite; and Jack Oliver, who would go on to play
a major fund-raising role for Bush/Cheney in 2000. I had no idea
why I had to be there. They were having this freewheeling political
discussion and I was looking around thinking, I despise everybody
in this room, as Israelite spoke feverishly about their pipe dream to
recruit retired general Norman Schwarzkopf to run as a Republican
for the Senate in Florida. This was unfortunate, because I've always
been the type of person who can't quite hide my contempt when I
think the person I'm talking to is a jackass.

Now all I could think was, Goddammit, I should have been
nicer to those guys.

Meanwhile, I was getting some very disturbing reports from inside the RNC. I had a conversation with Greg Strimple, a former
consultant to the RLC who was tight with Terry Nelson, the RNC's
political director. Strimple told me he'd been discussing the New
Hampshire situation with Nelson when Nelson said, "I've made sure
there's no e-mail traffic on this."

That could have meant, "I've checked to see if there's any e-mail
traffic on this, and there isn't." Or it could have meant, "I went and
found what e-mail traffic there was, and I've destroyed it."

I took it to mean there'd been a search-and-destroy mission for
evidence at the RNC. Why would I put it past them?

The DOJ finally charged me in early June. One count, conspiracy
to commit phone harassment. I could be sentenced with anything
from no time and a petty fine to five years in prison and a fine of
$250,000. Everyone I knew said there was no way I'd get whacked
with actual jail time, but I didn't share their confidence. So many
people were so incensed about the phone jamming that there was

no way I could see any judge letting me walk. Plus, as the first person in the jamming case that was going to be cutting a deal, I'd also be the first person getting sentenced, and that meant I'd be giving the judge his first opportunity to send a message.

On June 30, I was going to put on my pity outfit and return to the scene of the crime for my plea hearing. Elizabeth wanted to come to New Hampshire with me, but I told her I needed her to stay home.

"I should be there," she said. "Why don't you want me to be there?"

"Because we don't know what's going to happen and I'm treating this like any other business trip. I'm going up there, I'm having a meeting, and I'm coming home all on the same day. I don't want it to disrupt our lives, and I definitely don't want it to be emotional. I have to treat this like any other trip and not the potential ruining of our lives."

Eventually, she relented.

Everything was calm after that, until I got out of the shower and opened my underwear drawer.

"Honey," I said, "where are my plain white boxers?"

"I don't know—why do you need white boxers?"

"Because, in case I'm not coming home tonight, I don't want to go to jail wearing Speed Racer underwear."

She burst out laughing and said, "If there's one thing I never expected to hear my husband say, it's exactly that. At your fiftieth birthday party I'm mentioning this in my toast."

Even I had to smile at the preposterousness of it all. But more than that, I was smiling at the thought of my wife sticking around long enough to see my fiftieth birthday after I had turned our lives upside down.

Durkin picked me up at the airport and, on the drive to the courthouse, I must have found a dozen different ways to ask him, "Is there any way I'm going to jail today?"

Durkin devised just as many ways of saying "I don't see that happening"—none of them reassuring enough for me. Intellectually, I knew that even if I did get sentenced to prison, I wouldn't be sentenced at my plea hearing; I'd be given a date for a sentencing hearing. But there was so much anger toward me in New Hampshire that a judge there might just decide to forgo the usual formalities and lock me up pending sentencing. If he got it into his head that that was the thing to do, who was going to stop him?

So I was having a hard time playing it casual when we got to the courthouse, where I was expecting to be met by a mob of reporters asking questions and pissed-off patriots screaming for my hide. But it turned out that the DOJ was keeping things quiet; they'd kept my hearing off the public docket until late the previous day, so no one even knew I was coming except for an attorney for the New Hampshire Democratic Party. And the only press present was one guy from the Associated Press, thank God.

The proceeding itself flew by with all the emotion of a traffic court session. U.S. District Court Judge Joseph DiClerico read off the charge and asked Hinnen, "Does the government have anything to add?"

Standing, Hinnen said, "Mr. Raymond has signed the proffer and is going to be pleading guilty as far as we know today."

DiClerico then asked if I was Allen Raymond, if I understood the charges, and how I pleaded.

Yes, yes, and—"Guilty, Your Honor."

The judge set a sentencing date for the middle of July and dismissed us, but I had to stick around the courthouse to testify before a grand jury for the case against Jim Tobin. I went downstairs to a conference room, where I came face-to-face with an assistant U.S. attorney from the DOJ's New Hampshire office, Arnie Huftalen. So far, my case had been handled strictly by the Computer Crimes division of the DOJ's central office in Washington, D.C., but there was still a chance that they'd hand it off to the guys in New Hampshire to prosecute me. And this New Hampshire–based guy clearly couldn't stand the sight of me. Despite my crappy outfit, he was eyeing me like I was every inch the sleazy Republican fixer.

Durkin, who had known Huftalen for some time, asked him, "What do you think is the likelihood of incarceration for my client?"

"I think that's very remote," he said. "Nobody likes what happened, but I don't see anybody going to prison for this."

It was a huge weight off, like having a gravestone lifted off my face.

Okay, so the rest of the process was going to be unpleasant and expensive, but I was going to get through it without seeing—or smelling—the inside of a cell. I'd pay some fines, make some apologies, and start looking for a new line of work.

By the time Hinnen brought me into the courtroom where the grand jury was impaneled, I was starting to feel that the worst of my worries were behind me. I smiled and tried to look pleasant for the twenty or so New Hampshire citizens spread willy-nilly around the benches. This was just one of many cases they would be hearing that day.

After Hinnen finished asking me about the facts of the case, the jurors were free to ask questions of their own.

"Why did you take this work?" was the first thing they wanted to know.

They looked to me like homemakers and small businessmen, the kind of "Live Free or Die" folk who could appreciate the realities of turning over a buck.

"Look," I said, "you've got to understand that Jim Tobin and I had been colleagues and friends and then, after the Forbes campaign, we'd gone through a hiatus where we hadn't spoken at all in two years. Then in the summer of 2002 he first approached me about having the Republican Leadership Council give money to a congressional candidate who was also a personal friend of his up in Maine, which I did."

I explained how we had exploited election law by having one of my RLC donors who'd already given Tobin's candidate the legal limit give it to him all over again by sending it through the RLC, and added, "I was happy to do it—it happens all the time." Then I told them how Tobin had paid me back by sending some Maine business my way.

"So this was the new beginning of my relationship with the Republican National Committee. Tobin was their political director for New England, he'd been recognized as the RNC's guy in New Hampshire for seven years, so when he calls me about New Hampshire, I see him as the RNC."

Another juror asked, "Didn't it seem like the type of thing you should say no to?"

"Well, it certainly was unique, but, again, I saw this as the beginning of a new business relationship with the RNC, and I had fiduciary responsibility to my investors to take on all business—certainly all legal business, which is what I thought this was."

That's when a woman said to me, "When you say it was unique, did you talk to an attorney?"

Durkin and Hinnen had already advised me that I couldn't say I'd spoken to an attorney because I couldn't prove it and therefore couldn't use it as a defense.

So I looked at the woman, looked at Hinnen, and turned to the woman again. Nodding my head up and down, I told her, "I can't talk about that."

A juror in the back of the courtroom broke out laughing.

That was the end of my testimony.

Driving back to the airport, Durkin brought up my run-in with the DOJ's man in New Hampshire, telling me, "He isn't buying your act."

"As long as I'm not looking at jail time, he can buy or not buy whatever he wants. But what can you tell me about DiClerico? Can you read anything into that?"

"I can't tell you what he's thinking," replied Durkin, as visions of giant legal bills danced in my head.

The next morning, I woke up to stories in the *New York Times, Washington Post, Boston Herald,* AP–basically every daily paper or news service in the country–saying that I had pleaded guilty. CNN, CNBC, and FOX News were all running it as well. It was in the *Hill* and *Congressional Quarterly*'s Hotline, it was everywhere. I got calls from all over the country. People I hadn't heard from in years were ringing me up saying, "What the hell?"

Every article was bandying about that five-year, $250,000 maximum sentence. And every liberal blog was calling for me not merely to go to jail, but to get raped by the whole weight room once I got there. Raymond Buckley, the vice chairman of the Democratic Party in New Hampshire, casually compared phone jamming to murder. Despite my own work history, I considered it perverted to go to that extreme.

When I read Buckley's quote, even the assistant U.S. attorney's prediction that I wouldn't serve time lost all meaning. Buckley was using the same senseless, screeching, political rhetoric with which I'd long been so familiar. It reminded me that the actual facts of the crime could never be extricated from all the gamesmanship that had been heaped upon them–and that only a judge with no idea of, or interest in, the political machinations in his own jurisdiction would ever let me go without a prison sentence. And they don't make judges like that.

When I pleaded guilty, the DOJ had filed a request for leniency with the judge regarding sentencing because of my cooperation, but I knew that wouldn't necessarily count for much with the New Hampshire Democrats calling me a murderer.

I might have lost my shit completely, but Durkin had sat me down and explained the federal sentencing guidelines. Because of my status as a first-time, nonviolent offender, among other factors, my worst-case scenario was six months in prison and a fine to be determined by the judge. Still, despite all the people howling for blood, six months was a sentence I couldn't even contemplate at the time. It didn't seem rational to imagine that I could disappear from my life for that long and then return to it as if everything were normal again.

Chuck McGee was charged with three counts on July 9, 2004—all related to conspiring to make anonymous calls with the intent to annoy and harass. My sentencing hearing was scheduled for a few days later, but I was able to get it continued because, if I was going to serve time, the DOJ didn't want me sent up before they had brought Jim Tobin to trial—though, at the time, no one at the RNC knew Tobin would be charged; even Tobin didn't know.

On the 28th, McGee pleaded guilty.

After two years of lying through his teeth about me, he was finally confessing to what he'd done. It was a huge deal for my wife and me, a little vindication after two years alone in the political wilderness. We weren't jubilant, and we sure as hell were not out of the woods, but with McGee admitting that my version of the events had been true, the GOP would have to stop calling me a liar and a thief. I mean, with McGee pleading guilty, Tobin and his pals at the RNC would have to be completely out of their minds, total lunatics, to keep denying the truth, right?

Ever hear the one about the president who picked a land war in the Middle East? Or the one about the vice president who took a scattergun to an old man's face? And then got the old man to *apologize* for getting shot? That's the type I was dealing with.

— — —

Ever since my plea hearing, the New Hampshire Democrats had been pretty sure of Jim Tobin's involvement because Todd Hinnen had said in court that the government was pursuing an unnamed co-conspirator "from a national political organization." By October, just weeks before the presidential election, they were dying to get it into the papers. They figured that if they could link the phone jamming to the New England chairman of the Bush/Cheney campaign, the scandal would immediately leap from the local level to the proportions of a twenty-first-century Watergate. But they didn't have enough proof to go forward.

On the 13th, the Dems were set to depose a New Hampshire Republican Party official regarding the phone jamming. Twenty minutes before the scheduled start, the DOJ intervened with a court order stopping the deposition on the grounds that it would interfere with the ongoing criminal investigation. The Democrats screamed murder, which was a habit they were growing fond of.

Their play was "John Ashcroft's Department of Justice is interfering with this for political reasons!" Was that true? It may as well have been. Hinnen himself had told my lawyer that the case was being run directly from Ashcroft's office. And three weeks before the election, just when the Democrats were about to put someone under oath who might be able to establish that Bush/Cheney's man in the region had played a starring role, the DOJ rolled in and shut them down. With that, the New Hampshire Democrats had stood all they could stand—they could stand no more.

Kathy Sullivan got Democratic U.S. senators Patrick Leahy of Vermont and Ted Kennedy of Massachusetts to drop the bomb in a letter to Attorney General Ashcroft that read, "The last-minute timing of the Department's motion to intervene appears calculated to prevent the disclosure of information that might embarrass or implicate Tobin and possibly other Bush/Cheney campaign officials . . . and might also prevent injunctive relief to prevent unlawful campaign tactics in New Hampshire in the November 2, 2004, election."

The Democrats knew how to use their heavy hitters for optimum political impact as well as the GOP. Well, nearly.

Immediately Jim Tobin said, "I had nothing to do with this." But, pulling another strategy out of Chuck McGee's old playbook,

he resigned from the president's reelection campaign anyway, saying he didn't want to be a distraction.

Distractions were falling on swords all over the place!

Again it was in every paper. The biggest worry that Elizabeth
and I had was that all the name-calling would get into our home,
that some kid at school would wander up to Sam and say, "Hey,
your dad's a big criminal!"

But children are better behaved than the establishment behind
the Republican Party. The few people who decided to stick by me
were giving me regular reports on the rest of that pack. "What the
fuck is wrong with Raymond?" was the general refrain. "Why is he
doing this to Jim Tobin? What a scumbag!"

It was minion talk, the rank and file deciding that I was shit.

Graham Shafer, who had worked for Tobin and me simultaneously when we were together at the RNC, gave me his overview.
"It's the Tobin supporters. For instance, Blaise Lewis and Curt Anderson." Blaise Lewis I had handpicked to run the Pat Harrison
campaign, and Curt had thought well enough of me to recommend
me for job after job after job. It would have been one thing if they
thought I'd been lying about Tobin, but that's not what they thought
at all.

"Even if Jim is involved," Graham said, "people like Curt and
Blaise think you should have taken the fall. They think at the end of
the day, you're the vendor, you made the calls, you should be solely
responsible."

To which I explained: "Well, it doesn't fucking work that way.
That's coming from people who don't get it. Unless you're just a
total psycho who doesn't love your family, that's just not an option.
If it's between them and my family, they expect me to pick *them*?
They don't know what they're saying. They've never been in this
situation. So fuck those people. For all their What-Would-Jesus-Do?
wristbands, they're sure not acting like very good Christians."

The heart of what people like Blaise and Curt were saying was that, because Tobin had become more valuable to the Republican Party than I was, I should just roll over because the Party was what mattered above and beyond anything and anyone.

"What Party?" I posited with Graham. "There is no Party. It doesn't give you a gold watch when it's finished with you, there's no pension, and, by the way, I've got Republican congressmen in my own family going back to 1880 and I'm supposed to watch my family disintegrate for those pricks? Tell Tobin's boosters they can pound salt!"

In November 2004, Bush got reelected in another squeaker and took his "mandate" back to Washington to keep ruining whatever was left for him to ruin for another four years. Meanwhile, Tobin was left hanging in the wind until December 1, when he was indicted on four counts: two for conspiring to commit interstate communication without disclosing the caller's identity and with the intent to annoy and harass; and two counts for aiding and abetting the interstate phone harassment.

Oddly enough, by the time they finally charged him, I felt kind of ambivalent. I thought Tobin should certainly be indicted, but it was becoming less and less personal. Elizabeth and Durkin were an grier with him than I was. To this day, they say he set me up, that he knew I'd take the New Hampshire job when he dangled more RNC work before me; that the New Hampshire program was only a test run, a beta version of a new campaign strategy they intended to use in other close races—and that the RNC had dispatched Tobin to find a disposable non-Bushie to try it out with. After all, with Tony Feather and DCI running all the GOP phone work in every other state in 2002, why hadn't they gotten the New Hampshire job?

It took me a while to realize that it had been that much of a scheme. Even when Tobin was charged, I still saw it all as just a chain of mistakes. For a guy who was generally considered to be pretty smart, it certainly looked like I had been played like the proverbial grand piano.

Even though Tobin had betrayed me and I didn't like him, I was somewhat empathetic—not sympathetic. If there had ever been a human inside that Party automaton shell of his, it had taken a powder the instant he told me, "I have no idea what you're talking about." He would need every minute of what was about to happen to him before he'd ever get that humanity back.

Tobin pleaded not guilty on December 13. I couldn't believe it when I read it in the paper. This guy was tied to the rails with the train speeding toward him and all he was doing was whistling a happy tune. Did he think some Dudley Do-Right was coming to the rescue? He knew he was a conspirator, so what the hell else could he have been thinking?

Now, Tobin was not mentally defective; he could not have believed his own lies. So for Durkin, Elizabeth, and me, it came down to one question:

"Who is he protecting?"

The story in the paper was remarkable. When Tobin got up and said "I'm not guilty" the judge teed off on him, saying, "Mr. Tobin is no different than a street hooker. If he's guilty, I find his crime as offensive as any other crime."

I thought it was hilarious, and well deserved, and I was glad that that judge wasn't my judge.

Once Tobin had pleaded, I was all out of continuances. I had to show up for sentencing in New Hampshire on February 8, 2005. This time Elizabeth came, too, and we were holding on to each other throughout the flight as if our destination were the first circle of hell. When Durkin picked us up at the airport, he said, "I just can't see incarceration." But I had no faith left at all that I'd get off that easily.

Before we left our kids with Elizabeth's parents that morning, I had warned her, "I'm going to get time. I don't know how much, but it'll be something." I was hoping for three months home confinement, but I figured I'd end up having to spend half of it in prison.

The courthouse was crawling with reporters. Once Judge

DiClerico got things rolling, Todd Hinnen addressed the court, but didn't say much to give me hope. Hinnen dropped hints of more to come, saying, "We're pursuing coconspirators named and unnamed," but was mum as to the kind of sentence I should get.

This treatment was not lost on me. Hinnen was keeping my feet to the fire. They needed motivated cooperation and a vigorous testimony from me in Tobin's coming trial. They knew they could request a lighter sentence for me later on, but an easy one now might dull my willingness to be their main man under oath. They were playing with my life as only the government can; I was a piece on the board to be moved, or sacrificed, at the right time.

It was when Durkin spoke that things took that unfortunate turn I mentioned at the beginning of this story.

"As the government knows," he said, "my client did consult an attorney. However, he did not seek a written opinion but he did proceed with advice from—"

"Mr. Durkin, I'm going to stop you right there. What about common sense? What about a personal moral compass?"

It devolved from there. I mumbled about doing a bad thing and Kathy Sullivan read the riot act on behalf of the New Hampshire Democratic Party.

Elizabeth had been sitting in front of Sullivan and Paul Twomey, the New Hampshire Democrats' attorney. Before launching into her tirade, Sullivan had whispered to Twomey, "His wife is here. Do I really have to go that far?"

Yes, apparently, she did. And then the bailiff instructed me to stand before Judge DiClerico as he pronounced his sentence.

"Mr. Raymond," he said, "this is a serious crime. Regardless of your cooperation with the government, I find that it's appropriate that you serve a sentence of five months in prison."

Then he banged the gavel and dismissed the court.

It was all I could do to remain standing until he left the room. I fell back in my chair and I think I really would have collapsed, but then I remembered Elizabeth. I immediately strode to her, leaned over the railing, and pulled her into my arms, saying over and over again, "It's gonna be okay." I didn't really believe that, but I said it anyway—I had to say *something*.

A U.S. marshal sidled up to us. "I have to take Mr. Raymond in for processing," he told Durkin, and walked us down to the basement. We reached a steel door. The marshal unlocked it, told Elizabeth and Durkin they'd have to wait there, and walked me through to the other side.

Once he locked the door behind us, I asked, "Am I being processed into prison right now?"

"No," he said. "You'll get a date to report."

With that, he snapped my mug shot and took my fingerprints. My head was swimming. I honestly couldn't believe this was how I was ending up. How did a person with my advantages end up here, being processed for prison as a convicted felon? I didn't have many answers but one thing was painfully clear: there was no one to blame but myself.

The marshal unlocked the steel door again and returned me to the other side of it.

Durkin was white as a ghost—he hadn't seen this coming. When we got outside, he excused himself for a minute.

Alone with Elizabeth on the courthouse steps, I looked at my ink-stained fingers, then at my wife, and told her, "I don't think I can do this."

FIFTEEN

*B*efore we got home, Elizabeth and I stopped at our church and prayed with our priest. She was experienced in matters like mine, having been in Washington, D.C., since Watergate, when she provided spiritual comfort to some of those felons. Asking God to hook me up with a lighter sentence seemed like a bit of an imposition and, anyway, I'd already invested upward of a quarter million dollars toward that venture. So I prayed that my family would be okay. Then I let myself enjoy a few hours of life-sucking fear, depression, and a general, utterly crushing shell shock. After that, there were other things that demanded my attention.

John Durkin got me a continuance to stay out of prison until Jim Tobin's trial was finished; I was going to be testifying as the government's star witness in that trial, and I didn't want to arrive at my new digs without first getting credit for it. Meanwhile, my friends at the DOJ assured me that there would be a resentencing hearing between Tobin's trial and my prison reporting date.

About a month after DiClerico hit with me with my five-month sentence, on March 10, 2005, it was Chuck McGee's turn. DiClerico gave him seven months. That blew my mind. The difference between what I did in telling the truth and helping the government make its case and McGee's choice of spending two years lying, con-niving with his dark overlords to perfect the cover-up, and slander-ing a man every chance he got—the difference was two months. Two months. A bowl of Jell-O lasts longer. It wasn't even time enough for a boy band to go out of fashion.

But that wasn't the worst of it.

When Hinnen mentioned keeping McGee out of prison for Tobin's trial, the genius McGee insisted, "No. I want to serve my time now. I want to get it over with." The guy didn't even want to try for a sentence reduction; he couldn't get to jail fast enough. He was clearly taking a hit for the team, hoping the Godfathers would wel-come him back into the family when he came out the other side. Not that I cared about that, but his running off to serve that time was going to screw up my sentence reduction because if he'd already served seven months when I went in for my resentencing hearing, DiClerico would have to give me at least some time to scale with McGee's sentence. So, once again, my dreams of home confinement were soundly fucked out of existence.

Before shuffling off to a cell, McGee told the court, "I'm a good Catholic."

Perhaps I misunderstand Catholicism. But I believe that faith has some prohibition against falsely calling your fellow man a liar and a thief and never attempting to apologize for it. Given his recent behavior, I thought he should have spent a month in confession and then mow my lawn for a month as penance. By April, he was in a federal correctional institution.

A few months before the Tobin trial, Todd Hinnen was pulled off the Tobin case and given a White House job working for Condo-leezza Rice at the National Security Council. He was replaced by a couple of career guys, which did not bode well. If you haven't been promoted out of the DOJ after ten years or so, you're not quite the cream of the crop. From the moment I met the new prosecutors, Nick Marsh and Andrew Levchuk, I knew I was back at square one.

Levchuk was about six three, paunchy, and shaggy haired—and just *looked* like a big pain in the ass. Marsh had long vampire fingers and was the Robin to Levchuk's Batman. After all those months building a trustworthy working relationship with Hinnen, this pair from Keystone were making me out to be the villain all over again. And as far as the case itself was concerned, it was immediately apparent that they knew exactly nothing. When Durkin and I showed up for our first meeting, we saw no evidence that they had so much as read the file. I was shocked at how ill prepared they were. Moreover, I was completely uncomfortable with their understanding of the case. The DOJ had tacked a civil rights violation charge to the Tobin indictment and they wanted to make it stick even if they had to weld it to Tobin with a soldering iron.

Levchuk told me, "You prevented people from getting rides to polls."

"Maybe," I said, "but there is no constitutional right to a ride to the polls. I wasn't obstructing people's right to vote; I was obstructing a political party's ability to contact voters."

"What's wrong with your wiring? That's the whole point of the case."

"I don't see it that way."

Sick of me, Levchuk shook his head and stormed out of the room, followed closely by the Boy Wonder.

"You're hurting yourself," Durkin said.

"What do you mean? I've been honest."

"It's not about that anymore. They want that civil rights charge to hold up. You have to see it that way."

Then it hit me: I'm furniture. Federal law enforcement can turn you from a human being into a sofa left by the side of the highway if it wants to. The DOJ is just a blunt instrument that can get people to say or do anything; it smashes pegs of any size and shape into holes

of any size and shape without regard for the real dimensions of anything involved. It was not a nuanced approach. At least in the hands
of people like Levchuk and Marsh, the strategy was to rumble down
the middle, knock everything over, and then take what you wanted
from the scattered pieces.

"Look," I said to Durkin, "I just don't see it their way. You've got
to give me something to hold on to, a reason to say what they
want."

"Well, everything that happens on Election Day is all about getting out the vote. True?"

"Yes."

"And the phone harassment was aimed at closing down one way
of getting out the vote?"

"Fair enough."

"So," he reasoned, "you were making it harder for people to
vote. Can you live with that?"

"I suppose."

When Levchuk came back in, I said, "Here is what I can say
that's the truth, rather than what you want to hear."

None of it mattered anyway, as the judge in Tobin's trial ended
up tossing out the civil rights charge before a single witness ever
took the stand. Apparently Tobin's judge saw it my way, too.

Kathy Fuller, the FBI's investigator on the case, was there for
my second meeting with the new DOJ team in July 2005. Out of nowhere, Levchuk informed me, "You know, we've talked to a lot of
your former colleagues about you." He listed three people—Terry
Nelson, Chris LaCivita, and Mitch Bainwol—and then summed up,
"They said you have no integrity and can't be trusted."

With that, Levchuk said he had to take a call and walked out of
the room with Marsh. It was sort of devastating. I was offended that
all those people I'd worked with were suddenly ganging up on me.
Still, this was Washington, D.C. LaCivita was then working for DCI,
where Tobin was employed. Nelson, who had been the Bush/

Cheney 2004 campaign's political director, had been Tobin's boss at the RNC. Bainwol had been chief of staff to RNC Chairman Jim Nicholson and Tobin's RNC superior when I was chief of staff to RNC Cochairman Pat Harrison. We'd had some disagreements but nothing to warrant that kind of low favorability rating.

Once Levchuk and Marsh were out of the room, though, Kathy Fuller looked over, closed the door, and told me, "He's lying. Nobody said that about you—some of them even said very nice things."

So now I'm thinking, What's with the good cop/bad cop? They've already got me.

But it turned out that, in Kathy Fuller, I actually had an evangelist in the FBI. I think she went back to her counterparts at the DOJ and talked some sense into them, because they did begin treating me a little less like I'd beaten a fawn to death with a sack of kittens— though it did take some time.

Weirder things happened in the months leading up to the Tobin trial.

We lived at the end of a road that has a T section and a small cul-de-sac, just off a path that leads to the Capital Crescent Trail outside of D.C. So it wasn't unusual to see strange cars parked by our house while the owners were walking their dogs nearby. In fact, we'd gotten to know a number of the regular dog walkers and their cars.

But one day that spring we spotted an old green Subaru wagon with New Jersey plates across the street. The driver was slouched in the front seat, scribbling in a notebook. He'd scribble, observe our house, and then scribble some more. Elizabeth called the sheriff. The green Subaru beat it before the sheriff showed up, but he agreed that it was strange behavior and that Elizabeth was right to call it in since we had young children, but the mysterious note-taker went unidentified.

When I told Durkin about it, he said Tobin's defense team was sure to have hired private investigators to dig up dirt on me. Tobin had hired Williams & Connolly, the top white-collar defense firm in the country. Actually, the RNC had hired them, and were footing Tobin's legal bill, but I didn't know that little detail at the time.

The idea that these assholes were investigating me was annoying, but not frightening. What skeletons were they going to find? That I'd once been kicked out of a New England prep school for smoking weed? If they wanted to bring that, they were more than welcome, but I was pretty sure that type of activity was something several of the Bushies and even W. himself may have engaged in at some point.

A couple of months after the first clown with a notebook appeared, a second one followed. Elizabeth was walking Sam to the school bus stop when she noticed a middle-aged fatbody in a silver-gray sedan with Maryland plates watching the house and taking notes. Now that she could be pretty certain that our tubby voyeur was just some boozy dropout from one police department or another, rather than a psychopath with designs on our kids, she wanted to go up and ask him just what the hell he thought he was doing. But Sam admonished her about talking to strangers, so she kept walking.

When she came back from the bus stop the guy was gone, but a few minutes later he circled past our house again before taking off for good. She didn't bother with the sheriff that time.

A few weeks later, our garbage disappeared. I know, I say, "They stole our garbage" and it screams "Feeble conspiracy theory run amok," but events say otherwise. Our trash got picked up on Friday mornings, so by midweek the can on the curb was pretty full. One Tuesday afternoon, Elizabeth asked me if I'd taken out any garbage in the last few days. I said that of course I had, since we averaged five or six bags a week.

"Well," she said, "there's no garbage in the can."

We both wrote it off until Elizabeth asked a neighbor of ours who was in the CIA if it was common practice for investigators to make off with people's refuse. The response was, "Absolutely. That's CIA 101."

After that, we got in the habit of shredding all documents, stuffing them in bags, and keeping them in the basement. When we finally threw out the shredded paper after Tobin's trial, it took two months of weekly pickups to empty the basement.

And all throughout the eight-month period preceding the Tobin trial, every phone in our house would make strange clicking noises whenever we used them. Even my mother-in-law noticed it. All I know is, it stopped right before Tobin's trial started.

The last thing that happened before the big show was the revelation that the RNC was paying for every cent of Tobin's defense. At the time this was reported, they had already shelled out $750,000, and they would eventually spend more than $3 million defending Tobin. The reason, according to an RNC spokesperson, was that "Jim is a longtime friend and has served as both an employee and an independent contractor for the RNC." Either Tobin knew things that the Republican elite wanted him to keep his yap shut about, or he was just the sweetest little thing they'd ever seen.

RNC chairman Ed Gillespie first told the press that he had made the decision after consulting the White House. But implicating the Bush/Cheney White House was a thing unbecoming to any Republican who didn't wish to be reduced to bloody hunks for use as fertilizer at a certain Crawford, Texas, ranch. So, the next day, Gillespie remade his explanation and told the press that he had made the decision unilaterally and let the White House know about it afterward.

Now, that begged the question—why would the chairman of the RNC let the White House know about a decision he had made after he made it, when he didn't even need the White House's permission to make the decision in the first place?

I find that one answer serves to satisfy so many questions about the incongruities of Bush's top brass during that stunning era: they lie.

They lie when they're in trouble, they lie when they're safe; they lie when threatened, they lie when they are threatening; they lie about lies, they lie about lying about lies. And if they should happen upon some harmless, well-meaning little truth lying around, they beat it about the face and head until it *looks* like a lie, and *wants* to be a lie, and finally *does* become a lie. And people say there are no men of vision in Washington.

— — —

Jim Tobin's trial began in Concord, New Hampshire, on December 6, 2005. Marsh and Levchuk didn't know when I'd be called to testify, so they put me up in a Comfort Inn outside of Concord and left me there. Elizabeth stayed home because she couldn't leave the kids for days at a time, I couldn't rent a car because the DOJ didn't want me getting any farther from the motel than I could walk in the dismal New Hampshire slush, and I wasn't allowed to read the papers or watch the news. So I had brought a ton of books and prepared myself to watch a lot of HBO. I ordered a pizza my first night because there weren't any restaurants in walking distance, and it showed up cold and sopping wet. After that, I ate all my meals out of a gas station mini-mart.

The only place where I could get decent cell phone reception was in the parking lot, so twice a day, I'd take a break from pay-per-view, go out into the freezing cold, and check in with my wife.

When I finally got to testify, a briefing at the courthouse before I took the stand revealed that Marsh and Levchuk still hadn't done all their homework on the case.

"Is it just me," I asked Durkin when we were alone, "or are they not doing a very good job?"

"It's not just you. I hope they have a plan that we don't know about."

The one useful bit of information I picked up from Marsh and Levchuk was that Tobin was portraying himself as the victim. He was trying to place the connection between McGee and me on Chris Wood, a man who had nothing whatsoever to do with the phone jamming, but had the misfortune of knowing all the players involved because he'd worked for the Steve Forbes campaign in New Hampshire when Tobin and I had been on it. It was ironic for Tobin to say he was the victim by completely victimizing a totally innocent person. But it was also par for the course. So much for the Republican creed that an individual should take personal responsibility for his or her actions—and that victimization is for pussies.

Tobin, though, had gone beyond just pointing the finger. He and his attorneys at Williams & Connolly had drafted a flowchart replete with circles and lines that resembled something like a distorted Republican Family Tree with Chris Wood dead center of the controversy. Tobin wasn't just hiding from blame, he was actively seeking to send a totally innocent man to prison in his stead.

Then again, claiming to be a victim while making victims of the innocent is a strategy that has such a Rove-ish reek to it that I have to consider that it came straight from the RNC. After all, when a drug trafficker hires a lawyer for a mule who gets busted with five or six kilos of Peruvian jammed up his ass, it's not the mule who dictates legal strategy. The RNC wasn't likely to be shelling out $3 million for Tobin's defense team so that Tobin could call the shots.

Durkin left the little conference room where I was waiting to testify, peeked into the courtroom, and told me Chuck McGee was on the stand. A few minutes later, McGee walked into the conference room and grabbed a coat. He had already finished his sentence and was as thin as a rail. I just looked at him and shook my head. As he turned and left, I said to Durkin, "Prison must be a hell of a weight loss program."

Marsh came back in and asked, "Are you ready?"

"Yeah."

"How is it going?" Durkin said.

"McGee was a bad witness. It's clear he's looking for salvation with the Party and wants to be welcomed back. He's trying to deflect this off Tobin."

With his sentence served, the DOJ had nothing to hang over McGee's head. So he'd gone in and done all he could to take weight off Tobin, though he could only go so far without being charged with perjury. Now my testimony was even more important.

Right before I went to take the stand, the court broke for recess and I headed for the bathroom. The second I opened the door, I was standing eye to eye with Jim Tobin. Neither of us said a word or flashed an expression. We just walked past each other. I thought that was appropriate, since his legal defense was to pretend he barely knew me.

When I took the stand, I was eyeing Tobin along with his wife, Ellen, who was sitting behind him. They were both glaring at me. I held my head up a little higher. I can't say I wasn't nervous, but the collective stink-eye of Mr. and Mrs. Tobin had nothing to do with it. The RNC had provided Tobin with the best lawyers in the world, and I knew they had had me thoroughly vetted.

At one point early in the government's direct examination, Marsh asked me what I had discussed in one of my phone calls with Tobin just before Election Day. This was something I'd gone over again and again during my DOJ interviews, but I suddenly felt overwhelmed and my brain froze up. "I'm sorry," I said. "I'm drawing a blank. I'm sorry."

Meanwhile, Tobin and one of his lawyers, Dane Butswinkas, kept giving me dirty looks, as if that were going to intimidate me. But when I recounted how Tobin had said "I have no idea what you're talking about," I looked at Ellen Tobin and I swear I saw a flicker of doubt in her eyes.

Man, I thought, that has got to sting.

"If Jim Tobin had never called and asked you to do this job," Marsh asked, "would you have done it?"

I could expound on the topic or be brief. I went with a simple "No." It turned out McGee had said the exact same thing when asked that question.

Marsh also brought up the Super Bowl calls I had made for Jim Treffinger during the 2002 GOP Senate primary campaign. Butswinkas immediately objected. In a sidebar, he complained to the judge that my prior "bad acts" had no relevance. It may sound counterintuitive that the defense attorney for the man my testimony was aimed against wouldn't welcome evidence of my bad acts—but Butswinkas knew where Marsh was going.

The judge asked how the Super Bowl calls were relevant and Marsh argued that they established that I was publicly known as a "player" involved with "an aggressive ad" that ended up getting me interviewed by the feds.

"Why does the jury need to know that?" the judge asked.

"Because it explains why the referral to this guy, rather than somebody else. It tends to make that the more-likely-than-not route."

As the judge put it, Marsh was trying to establish that I had "a dirty reputation" and that that was why Tobin had chosen me for the New Hampshire program. Again, blunt object. Marsh was ignoring everything I had told the feds about being out of the RNC business ever since Tony Feather and DCI had put their stranglehold on it, in favor of the absurd notion that a guy I had worked with for years chose GOP Marketplace for the New Hampshire program based on one minor operation in a New Jersey primary. Furthermore, Marsh was choosing to ignore simple logic, because that's how the government prosecutes. Marsh wanted to simultaneously paint me as the stand-up guy the jury could believe because I'd acknowledged my sins, *and* as a dirty political trickster with a wide reputation as such, which was why Tobin called me and no one else.

The objection was sustained.

On his cross-examination, Butswinkas asked me about pricing the New Hampshire calls, saying, "You had discussions with Mr. Raymond about how much it was going to cost, how much you were going to charge, isn't that right?"

"Well, I'm Mr. Raymond, so yes."

"Ah, that's a fair point. You got me on that one."

I wanted to say, "You're the only one playing gotcha," but I didn't want to come off as a wiseass. I was employing the George

Costanza theory of "Doing the Opposite of Every Instinct to Come Out on Top."

Butswinkas seemed nervous. I had been expecting Clarence Darrow or Perry Mason, but this guy was more like Lionel Hutz on *The Simpsons.* If I were Tobin, I'd have been freaking out watching Butswinkas stumble through his papers muttering, "Umm," and "But," and "Gimme a minute." He'd say, "I want to ask you a question," and then reverse himself with, "Umm, no, I don't want to ask you that question." Many of the courtroom spectators were local attorneys who wanted to see a Williams & Connolly man in action; they must have been glad they hadn't paid for the performance.

His initial line of attack was to paint me as a rich GOP insider that no one should have any sympathy for.

"You said on direct [examination] that this was really important to you because you were a small-business person, right?"

"That's correct."

"And you were trying to give the jury the impression that you were the little guy and this big guy from the RNC was calling you, right?"

"No, that's not."

"What were you trying to give them the impression of?"

"I owned a small business and I was looking for more business."

"Well, you weren't really a little guy back then, were you?"

"I was a small-business man," I said. "I ran a small business. I don't know what 'little' means. If you could describe that to me, I might be able to answer your question."

"Well, okay," he said, "I will." But he never did. "Isn't it a fact that between January of 2001 and December of 2002, you did almost two million dollars of business?"

"Yes. I was very proud of that."

"Is that what you meant by small business when you were testifying?"

"We're less than two employees, so I think that qualifies as a small business, yes."

"That's pretty good, isn't it?"

"Those are gross numbers, not profit." Such distinctions seemed to be lost on Butswinkas, so I explained, "The funds that you're referring to on the customer summary which I provided to you at your request—"

"At my subpoena."

Now, I know that lawyers are paid to be argumentative asses, but this ass *really* couldn't stop himself arguing.

"Yes," I said, "you requested that I give it to you and I was glad to."

"You gave us this document in response to a subpoena, didn't you?"

"Yes, you asked for the document through a subpoena and I gave it to you."

In his continued effort to paint me as the ultimate D.C. shadow man, Butswinkas then spent about ten minutes just listing and identifying the twenty or so current and former Republican governors, U.S. senators, and members of the House whose names appeared on RLC stationery as its "Advisory Committee" when I was executive director. I pointed out that they had nothing to do with the daily operations of the organization.

"Did you get a six-figure salary from this organization?" he asked.

"Yes, I did."

"In October 2002, things were going very well for you, weren't they?"

"Yes, they were."

"You had this six-figure position that we just talked about?"

"Yes."

"And your company, GOP Marketplace, was earning about a hundred and thirty percent return on the investment?"

"Yes, I'm very proud of that."

Now that he'd gotten in a few words about my wealth, Butswinkas wanted to paint me as down-at-the-heels desperate.

"But at the time you decided to cooperate with the government," he said, "things had taken a turn for the worse, hadn't they?"

"Well," I replied, "things have certainly changed."

Butswinkas tried a little jab there, saying, "They should have." I made no reaction, and he pushed forward with, "You had lost that six-figure salary, right?"

"Yes, I have."

"You would say that would be a turn for the worse, right?"

He was dead set on getting me to accept his definition of my circumstances, on having me define myself for the jury with his words.

"Well," I said, "it was a loss of income."

"Your company has essentially gone out of business, right?"

"GOP Marketplace was *put* out of business, yes."

"You would say that was a turn for the worse, wouldn't you?"

"Certainly a change in circumstances."

"Just a change of circumstances?" At that, he mustered up that kind of lawyer outrage that looks so good in movies and never quite plays in real life. Then he flipped his silly lid. "You're the president of this company that made two million dollars in two years and it went out of business—that's a change in *circumstances*? Not a turn for the worse? Is that what your honest—what do you take these folks for?" By "these folks" I assumed he meant the jury.

As Marsh objected, and before the judge could rule, I answered, "Citizens of New Hampshire."

The objection was sustained and Butswinkas withdrew the statement, muttering, "I'm sorry, Your Honor."

The next case he tried to make was that I would say anything the government wanted me to in exchange for leniency. That line of questioning went on for several seasons. I kept explaining that I had only agreed to tell the truth, so that Butswinkas might understand me. I found several novel ways of structuring my answers to that end, but his English was a little faulty. At one point, I admitted that, obviously, "I would rather not spend five months in prison."

Butswinkas jumped on that: "You'd rather stick Mr. Tobin there instead of you, right?"

"No."

"But you realize that's how it works, don't you?"

"Mr. Tobin is on trial here. He is in a situation because he's in a situation. I'm very empathetic, but all I've been asked to do, and all I've done, is tell the truth."

It was a very poignant moment for me—most people wait all their lives for a perfect opportunity to declare, "I'm not the one on trial here!" but only one in ten thousand ever gets it.

Butswinkas knew he was done. He was clearly playing to the jury and they just weren't buying his act. On top of that, the guy just would not stop talking. Most people won't listen to the president of the United States for more than twenty minutes at a stretch, and Butswinkas's cross-examination of me lumbered on for five and a half hours without the slightest reference to sex or violence for the jurors to latch on to. By the end of that stirring spectacle, Butswinkas was red in the face and shaking his fist at me—and one of the jurors was sound asleep.

I was sipping water from a paper cup as I left the stand. When I walked past Butswinkas and Tobin at the defense table, I put a little spring in my step, crushed the cup in my hand, and tossed it in their wastebasket.

A week later, Tobin was convicted on two counts. At sentencing, the court gave him ten months and let him stay out on bail pending an appeal. The appeals court later reversed the convictions and Tobin headed back to court for another trial.

He was finally out of my life.

I started getting ready for prison.

— — —

Ever since I broke my nose playing rugby as a kid, I had been a horrible snorer. I figured prison was going to be bad enough without getting my ass kicked every night for keeping my fellow convicts awake with beastly noises, so I went in for septum surgery. I highly recommend this for felons and innocents alike—I've slept like a lamb ever since.

Reading up on life in a federal correctional institution, I discovered that their guests are issued not very supple steel-toed boots. I had bad arthritis in my right ankle, so I got that fixed with surgery, too.

Along the way, I gave up chewing tobacco and caffeine so that my time wouldn't be further aggravated by physical cravings.

Physically, a little low-security fed time is just the prescription for fortysomethings who are stubborn about getting in shape.

The usual crowd was on hand for the resentencing hearing on February 2, 2006. Aside from Durkin, Elizabeth, and me—and Marsh and Levchuk—the New Hampshire Dems again showed their presence with chairman Kathy Sullivan and their attorney, Paul Twomey.

I didn't know what DiClerico would elect to hit me with this time around, but I did know one thing for certain—I wasn't going to fuck up like I had the last time. After the first sentencing, when I had told Elizabeth, "I don't think I can do this," it had really scared her. Whatever happened, I wasn't going to lose it again, at least not in front of my wife.

My resolve not to fuck up was not contagious, however. Marsh started doing that the second he opened his mouth in front of the judge. He was there to request a lighter sentence, but all the guy seemed capable of saying was, "Mr. Raymond is guilty . . . Mr. Raymond did a bad thing."

I wanted to tell Durkin to make him shut the hell up and sit down. He was killing me. After about five minutes of torching my ass, he realized his mistake and paused to figure out how to undo the damage. Levchuk didn't give him a chance, just put a hand on Marsh's shoulder and said, "I'll take it from here." At that point I didn't know what Levchuk was going to say, but at least Marsh had stopped talking, and that was something.

Addressing DiClerico, Levchuk said, "Your Honor, Mr. Raymond was a tremendous witness, and he was a tremendous cooperating witness, because he didn't tell us what he thought we wanted to hear—he told us the truth. And that's the best kind of witness you can have. Because their candor, their honesty, is evident when they're on the witness stand. It's undeniable. The jury can see that this is someone who is telling the truth. The jury saw that in Mr. Raymond."

Levchuk closed with "Because of his unparalleled cooperation, we are asking for three months of home confinement."

Next, Durkin got up and did his thing: "My client has lost his livelihood, he's lost his career. He's lost the ability to vote, which, obviously, for someone who's worked in public service and in the election process, that's a severe punishment. Mr. Raymond, having lost everything that he's ever worked for, that should be punishment enough. We ask that you let him go home, per the government's request."

DiClerico then handed it off to me. This time I was actually prepared. "The first thing I'd like to do, Your Honor, is apologize to my wife, who's stood by me—thank God. I couldn't have gotten through any of this without her. Thank you, Elizabeth." I turned around and looked at Elizabeth for a moment.

Then I continued, "I would also like to apologize to the citizens of New Hampshire, to the Manchester Fire Department, and the state's Democratic Party." It pained me to apologize to the Democratic Party—how they could equate my crime with murder in the press and still consider themselves any different than the Republicans is a question only a politician would ever be fanatical enough to tackle, but I was willing if it kept me out of jail.

"This was very bad judgment," I started my close, "but I take full responsibility, and I have since the beginning. When our government came to me and asked me what happened, I didn't hesitate to tell them the truth. I'm the only person in this whole process that never hesitated to tell the truth. And I ask the court to take this into consideration before making its ruling."

Despite everything that was said, I knew the judge still had to consider the dynamic that was created when Chuck McGee had skipped off to jail to enroll in his federally sponsored Jenny Craig program. After doing some quick math, he said, "I find that the defendant should serve three months incarceration. That is a forty percent reduction off his sentence, which I find fair. So ruled."

With that, the gavel came down, and I could look forward to a superextended spring break at the federal correctional institution in scenic Loretto, Pennsylvania.

I heard Elizabeth break out in a sob, so I went to grab her. She was stoic, but this was hard. As soon as I had her in my arms, Paul Twomey whispered in her ear, "It's okay, my brother served time there—it's a safe place."

"I can do this," I told her. "We can do this. It's three months low-security, it's nothing. I've been away on campaigns longer than that. We can do this."

So I did it. After ten full years inside the GOP, ninety days among honest criminals wasn't really any great ordeal.

EPILOGUE

Felo de Se

I was inside the Federal Corrections Institution in Loretto, teaching a muscle-bound convict his ABC's, when I learned the most stirring lesson of all. The convict, Mr. Mack, was a bit too agitated that particular afternoon to focus on his reading because some gym equipment had broken and could never be replaced thanks to a federal law the inmates had named "The Zimmerman Amendment."

Here's what my fellow prisoners didn't know, and what I sure as hell never shared with them: "The Zimmerman Amendment" was actually a law authored as "The No Frills Prison Act" and rammed through congress in 1996 by Representative Dick Zimmer of New Jersey—my former boss at the Republican Leadership Council. Dick had been laying the foundation for a Senate candidacy and chose to target the U.S. prison population as his whipping boy. In one release, Zimmer stated, "We shouldn't be using taxpayer dollars to turn prisons into vacation spas." Later, Zimmer criticized prisons that boasted "weight rooms, softball fields, and microwave ovens."

It had made for good campaigning; I even used it in direct mail ads to bolster the tough-on-crime posture of some of my own candidates. But alone there in a prison classroom with a rather large, pissed-off felon who hadn't been able to relieve any of his stress or aggravation on the weight pile that day, I realized that all the bullshit guys like me peddle out on the campaign trail actually comes to pass if we get our candidates elected. Our promises, our phony wedge issues, our polarizing rhetoric—it can all come true, it can all happen. And it all happens to real-life human beings.

The problem is, laws are not often drafted and passed by real-life human beings. Laws are handed down by people who haven't lived in real life for many years. Once you have the power to make laws or influence their making, you've entered into a realm where the law doesn't seem to apply to you anymore. Nixon said that if the president does it, it's not illegal. Well, if a legislator or the people behind him do something, how can *that* be illegal? They don't break laws, they make laws.

By the time I committed my own crime—though I may not have been fully conscious of it—it didn't seem like anything an electioneer did could be against election law because, hey, we were the guys who made that stuff up in the first place.

Being run through the sausage machine that is our justice system firmly proved to me the veracity that "law is King." Thomas Paine called it in 1776 when he penned that phrase in *Common Sense* and, while it's truer now than ever, it also assumes a purity of law that no longer exists in this country. In the Bush 43 administration, with a complicit Republican Congress, America saw the executive branch expand existing laws as a way to make new laws.

My own case is an example of this, borne out by the ruling of the First Circuit Appellate Court in Jim Tobin's appeal. The court reversed and remanded the case, acknowledging that Jim Tobin was involved as a key player in the phone jamming: "That Tobin assisted in the substantive crime is patent; his call to Raymond was integral to the accomplishment of the scheme." But to the point, the appellate court also said, "In sum, we think that to equate harassment with any repeat calling done in bad faith is to enlarge the scope of the statute."

This has been the Bush 43 administration's secret sauce: enlarging the scope of various statutes to tip the checks and balances scale in favor of the executive branch. Take wiretapping surveillance, the Guantánamo Bay detainees, interpretation of the Geneva Conventions, abuse of the signing statement, the White House/RNC e-mail Freedom of Information Act controversy, the firing of U.S. attorneys with fabricated cause, and—uniquely illustrative—Vice President Dick Cheney's boggling assertion that his office does not exist in either the executive or legislative branch of government, and is therefore not bound by the rules of either one.

Of course, you can't lay it all on Bush's doorstep. This November, the American people may very well enter into the twenty-first through twenty-fifth years of unfettered two-family rule—completely of their own free will. If it happens, historians will be able to illustrate a quarter century of American politics thus: Bush-Clinton-Bush-Clinton. How did we get here? Because election operatives like myself and the kind of politicians who hire us have ensured that idealists can't win elections. Only the cynics are making the laws.

They get in power, they stay in power, and they keep the power. But don't the voters have some power in this mess? Sure. And they give it up every election.

Common Sense has come full circle: "For as in absolute governments the King is law, so in free countries the law ought to be King." The question every American should be asking as they try to assess the current presidency, and decide on the presidential election with the potential for a Clinton 44 administration, is a simple one: Is the law King, or is the King the law?

You're the voter, so my hope is that this advice will help you figure things out for yourself. This book offers the unvarnished truth—chaste, plain, forthright, and untouched by politicians, lobbyists, and partisan hacks. Question the tone and message of the next piece of political mail you receive, the next radio spot, the next telemarketing call, the next ad on television, the Internet, the newspapers, everything. Now you speak the language, or at least enough to get around; enough to be dangerous to those who think they can dupe you.

That is everything I can tell you from the inside—how the system is used by people just like me, in both parties, and that they are paid to win at all costs. The tactics will only get tougher, nastier, more brutal, because the tricks of the trade are known, embellished upon, and passed forward by people like me to *more* people like me, with the competition growing stiffer and the stakes rising higher with every election. So there it is.

Now, what are you going to do about it?

ACKNOWLEDGMENTS

My wife, Elizabeth, has been the foundation without whom this book, and everything that is good in my life, would not be. My sons, Samuel and William, whom I love deeply, have shown great support in ways they do not yet understand. I am grateful for my longtime and dear friend Peter Aronson, without whom this book would not have happened and would not be as great. Many thanks to Joe Regal, literary agent-in-chief who shared the vision and had the daring to make sure this book was published. Thanks to David Rosenthal for making this book happen, and to Dedi Felman for her skill and encouragement. The support and provision of my father, and Warren, Lyn, Daniel, Anne, and David and Darwin deserve credit. Without them the journey would have been much harder for all of us. And to Ian, a remarkable talent, thank you!

ABOUT THE AUTHORS

ALLEN RAYMOND is a former top GOP operative who served time in federal prison for the phone jamming operation during the 2002 New Hampshire elections. He spent nearly a decade working to elect Republican candidates, first at the state and then the national level.

He is currently a business development consultant and a trustee of a charitable foundation. Raymond is married to Elizabeth Sherman, and they have two sons.

IAN SPIEGELMAN spent four years as a reporter for the *New York Post* and has been a staff writer for *New York* magazine and a contributing editor for *Details*. He is the author of two novels, *Everyone's Burning* and *Welcome to Yesterday*, and recently coauthored *Cooked: From the Streets to the Stove, From Cocaine to Foie Gras* with chef Jeff Henderson.